D1625742

☆

6| 2186432

# Traces of

# **Peter Rice**

edited by
**Kevin Barry**

THE LILLIPUT PRESS

First published 2012 by
# THE LILLIPUT PRESS LTD
62–63 Sitric Road, Arbour Hill, Dublin 7, Ireland
www.lilliputpress.ie

ISBN 978 1 84351 386 5

A CIP record is available from the British Library.

1 3 5 7 9 10 8 6 4 2

Set in 10.5 on 14.5 pt Garamond
Design by Niall McCormack
Printed and bound in England by MPG Books, Bodmin, Cornwall

# CONTENTS

Traces of
# Peter
# Rice

Peter Rice was inspiring not just because of his brilliance as an analyst, but because he was driven by a commitment to pushing the boundaries of his discipline of structural engineering. Never satisfied with the status quo, he continued to explore the innovative use of materials throughout his life: 'the search for the authentic character of a material is at the heart of any approach to engineering design' (*An Engineer Imagines*, p. 78). Although he described himself as a dreamer with a love of numbers – a label that could safely be used for a lot of engineers – his approach to projects was also collaborative and humanistic.

Rice established his reputation during the late 1970s and through the 1980s at a time when engineers were working with increasingly sophisticated computer technology. Were it not for his untimely death in 1992, he would no doubt have continued to integrate state-of-the-art systems into his own practice. Yet he also had an understanding and love of craftsmanship, whether the work of the Moroccan stonemasons who constructed the dry stone walls of the Full-Moon Theatre at Gourgoubès, in the Languedoc – a project which used no mechanized processes – or the skill of the master plasterer who shaped the sprayed ferro-cement leaves in a single, continuous application for the roof profile of the Menil Collection museum, Houston, or the cast steel of the gerberettes, finished by hand, which were to become the icon of the design for the Centre Pompidou in Paris. Throughout his career Rice valued testing and prototyping, often using handmade models, including for the three aforementioned projects. This element of Peter Rice's work as well as the collaborative process of evolving a design are explored in the exhibition *Traces of Peter Rice*.

The exhibition is complemented by a film and this book, which brings together memories by friends and associates of Peter Rice, who, twenty years after his death, have opportunity to reflect upon his life and work. Rice's close working relationships with colleagues like Tom Barker at Arup, as well as the extraordinary partnership with his peers in the field of architecture Richard Rogers and Renzo Piano, and the later establishment of his own firm Rice Francis Ritchie (RFR) in Paris with Ian Ritchie and Martin Francis, are well documented. Less well known is that he enjoyed working with young graduates whom he gathered around him to cut their teeth on major projects. 'It was sink or swim, probably like his own experience on the Sydney Opera House', said Sophie Le Bourva, who first started working with Rice at the age of twenty-three years and who went on to engineer the second Pompidou Centre in Metz designed by Shigeru Ban. 'But Peter ensured that most of us swam.'

Rice had, in his early career, been on the design team for the Sydney Opera House. He persuaded Jack Zunz, Senior Partner at Arup, to send him to Sydney as site engineer where Jørn Utzon, architect of the Opera House, was to have a lasting impact on the young engineer: 'I would follow him around site and listen to him reasoning and explaining why he had made certain decisions. The dominant memory was of the importance of detail in determining scale, in deciding the way we see buildings.'

The photograph on the jacket of this book shows Peter Rice at a meeting in 1990 with Japanese architect Yutaka Saito. By this time, Rice was renowned in the world of architecture, with stars of that firmament clamouring for his attention. The model in the background of the photograph was nicknamed 'the hairy wok' because of the steel roof sprouting bushes as hair. The project for a studio was relatively modest and small scale (no more than 20m x 10m), but that that did not deter Rice from giving his time to participate in the design session. For him, ideas were key.

*Traces of Peter Rice* opens in London in November 2012 and tours in May 2013 to Paris and the following autumn to Dublin. Its form and content will respond anew to the character of each venue. Workshops and conferences will be organized in all three cities. This is the last exhibition of the current programme at Arup in London by Phase 2, which presents and produces multi-disciplinary exhibitions and events globally. Since 2008 the London space has been used for the exploration of innovative ideas and cross-disciplinary exchange between the fields of architecture, engineering, art and design. *Traces of Peter Rice* is a fitting exhibition for the Phase 2 programme since Peter Rice personified its agenda through the way he worked, the boldness of his projects and his passion for life.

The three parts of this project, exhibition, film and book, owe much to Peter Rice's family: Sylvia, Kieran, Julia, Heidi, Nemone and Nicki, and to his siblings Maurice Rice and Kitty Gibney. I am indebted to them for their generosity and willingness to share memories and personal collections.

The contributors to this book have created a fantastic tribute to Peter Rice. I thank Kevin Barry, who has edited this diverse range of texts so capably, Henry Bardsley, Barbara Campbell-Lange, Ed Clark, Hugh Dutton, Martin Francis, Jonathan Glancey, Peter Heppel, Sophie Le Bourva, Amanda Levete, J. Philip O'Kane, Seán Ó Laoire, Renzo Piano, Ian Ritchie, Vivienne Roche, Richard Rogers, Andy Sedgwick, and Jack Zunz. Thanks also to Antony Farrell and all at The Lilliput Press, Dublin, for pulling out the stops to meet our publishing deadline, and to Niall McCormack for the elegant book design.

3

The film, which offers an illuminating new portrait of Peter Rice and a valuable record for future studies, is the work of Ben Richardson. Its completion would not have been possible without the assistance of Taghi Amirani, Piers Dennis, Kelsey Eichhorn, Will Fewkes and Chris Wanklyn. Thanks to all who gave their time to be interviewed.

Invaluable to our project was the advice of many of Peter Rice's past associates: Laurie Abbott, Henry Bardsley, André Brown, Humbert Camerlo, Barbara Campbell-Lange, Mike Davies, Mike Dowd, Hugh Dutton, Martin Francis, Lennart Grut, Shunji Ishida, Peter Morice, Nicolas Prouvé, Ian Ritchie, Yutaka Saito, Alan Stanton, John Stanton, Frank Stella and Jane Wernwick. *Traces of Peter Rice* also benefitted from the guidance and help of the following colleagues at Arup: John Batchelor, Tristram Carfrae, Ed Clark, Bruce Danziger, Alistair Guthrie, Mitsuhiro Kanada, Keiko Katsumoto, Sophie Le Bourva, Rory McGowan, Andy Sedgwick and Pauline Shirley as well as that of former Arupians: Tom Barker, Brian Carter, Bob Cather, Bob Emmerson, John Thornton and Jack Zunz.

The exhibition was made possible through the close cooperation and generosity of the following lenders: Humbert, Viviane and Alexandre Camerlo; Mike Dowd; Martin Francis; Fondazione Renzo Piano; Sylvia Rice and Kieran Rice; Ian Ritchie and Frank Stella. Thanks also to Vicki MacGregor, Curator of Exhibitions at Rogers Stirk Harbour and Partners, and Jo Murtagh, assistant to Richard Rogers, for enabling access to archive material and liaising on our behalf with key people at the crucial time of planning the exhibition. Rozenn Samper at RFR and Stefania Canta and Chiara Casazza at the Renzo Piano Building Workshop provided excellent support in gathering together visual material.

Producing an exhibition like *Traces of Peter Rice* requires an intense collective effort. I am most grateful to Jeremy Leahy, Toria Richardson, Richard Roberts, Rob Updegraff and Nick Westby, who have been a terrific team to work with on exhibition design, build and installation over the four years of the Phase 2 programme and who have excelled in their work for this show. The beautiful pod, inspired by Peter Rice's collaboration with Humbert Camerlo on the Full-Moon Theatre, has been designed by Tristan Simmonds. Wolfram Wiedner has provided an inventive and captivating graphic design to weave the elements together. Diana Kovacheva, Ralph Wilson and Eva Xie deserve special thanks for assisting on the project with enthusiasm and resourcefulness. Jane Joyce, Ruby Kitching and Mark Whitby have been meticulous in their research towards creating a digital profile of Peter Rice for an online engineering timeline. I also thank Francesco Anselmo for adapting and reconfiguring the timeline software for the exhibition and for his computer programming for Phase 2 since 2008, and Philip O'Kane for taking on the task of digitizing Peter Rice's notebooks. *Traces of Peter Rice* would not have been possible without the encouragement and continuous support of Martin Ansley-Young, Chris Luebkeman, Andy Sedgwick and David Whittleton at Arup. I thank Philip Dilley, Chairman of Arup Group, under whose auspice Phase 2 was initiated.

This project is a collaboration between Arup, Culture Ireland, the Centre Culturel Irlandais, and the Irish Office of Public Works. I am immensely grateful to Sheila Pratschke, Director of the Centre Culturel Irlandais, to Mary Heffernan of National Historic Properties, to the team at Farmleigh Gallery, and to Kevin Barry, Professor Emeritus at the School of Humanities, National University of Ireland, Galway, whose dedication ensured that our collective endeavour was brought to fruition.

It is thanks to you all that the traces of Peter Rice endure.

Jennifer Greitschus
HEAD OF EXHIBITIONS, ARUP

Peter Rice at fancy dress parade c.1942.

# 1

# Memories of Peter

Maurice Rice

I was born in Dundalk shortly before the Second World War, some three and a half years after Peter. Life in an Irish provincial town was of course restricted during the war years and for some time after, but we were spared the terrible consequences that occurred elsewhere. My memories of this time are fragmentary. Our father was proud of the car that he bought shortly before the war. It sat in the garage on brick piles for many years. Peter and I would sneak in from time to time and pretend to drive it. When finally petrol became available, our father used it regularly to get out of the town and take walks in the countryside. Peter has written in *An Engineer Imagines* about these excursions to the woods near Ravensdale and the Irish Sea at Gyles Quay. We would spend the time building sand castles and competing on whose could withstand the incoming tide the longest. Driving in rural Ireland had other excitements like threading through flocks of cows or sheep and holding one's breath as chickens scurried home across the road when a car approached. These trips also allowed us to observe the Irish ability to accommodate all sides. As we passed a rural pub on a holiday, the front doors would be shuttered and closed in accordance with the law, but the car park would be occupied, indicating there were customers who had gone in through the back door.

This Irish trait was also very much in evidence during our schooling. Peter and I went to the Irish Christian Brothers School, which put emphasis on discipline and learning to do well in the state examinations. The Marist fathers ran the other nearby school. It had a more relaxed approach with pupils drawn from the sons of the local merchants etc. Peter started school there. However, we were from a family of teachers and our mother was determined that we would have a strict education, since there was no family business to inherit. So when she quizzed young Peter to see what he had learned, she was disturbed and the school was changed. The Christian Brothers went beyond the government's policy of one class per day of compulsory Gaelic for all schoolchildren and used Gaelic for all subjects, except English. The result was a disconnect between school in Gaelic and daily life in English. The outcome was predictable and the Gaelic revival did not spread beyond a committed minority. Neither Peter nor I developed much enthusiasm for the study of ancient sagas and mournful poems lamenting the sorrowful history of our country.

When the time came for university, our father made the unusual decision, especially for the 1950s, to send Peter to study engineering at the Queen's University in Belfast. He felt that Belfast, being an industrial city with a tradition in aeronautical and marine engineering, was a more appropriate choice than Dublin. Belfast at that time was a rather dreary place that largely shut down on Sundays in conformance with its dominant Presbyterian culture. Peter, however, was undaunted and had no reservations about entering fully into university life. He joined the rowing club and the university Air Squadron – a programme sponsored by the Royal Air Force to gain access to university undergraduates. When he visited home, he would regale us with stories about his adventures learning to fly in Chipmunk trainers. As the younger brother I was very impressed when he talked about his flying escapades, before being rescued each

Thomas 'Dada' Quinn with daughters and grandchildren at his home in Inishkeen,1946: Peter Rice *front left*, Maurice Rice *front centre*, his sister Kitty on 'Dada' Quinn's right; Maureen Rice stands behind her father, her husband James to her left with cigarette.

Peter Rice, 'Dada' Quinn, Aunt Nora, Kitty, Maurice c.1945

Peter and Maurice Rice, Dundalk 1942.

time by the instructor sitting behind him. As his studies drew
to an end, the trainees went to an RAF base to be exposed to
jet fighters etc. However, Peter decided not to pursue a career
in the RAF and preferred engineering, much to the relief of our
mother. Thinking back, the choice of Queen's was surely a good
one as it exposed Peter to aeronautical engineering and opened
him to a wider approach to novel and light structures than was
available in standard civil engineering.

After Peter moved to London and I was studying in
Dublin, our paths didn't cross until I moved to Cambridge
in 1960. Shortly thereafter Peter and Sylvia married and I was
an inexperienced best man. But the wedding went off well. It
was not a big affair, in keeping with the modest salaries paid to
engineers. They moved into a flat in Notting Hill Gate, which
at that time was starting to be gentrified. Peter was excited to be
working with Ronald Jenkins who he said was the best at Arup.
In the years that followed we lived far apart, he and his family
moved to Sydney and I to the United States.

Our next overlap was in the USA. After leaving Sydney he
spent a year decompressing at Cornell University from the stress
of working on the Sydney Opera House. I was living not too far
away in New Jersey, newly married. I remember well a weekend
together in Ithaca. It was winter and very cold in upstate New
York. Peter and Sylvia had three young children by then and
were living in a large old wooden house. Helen and I were
overwhelmed by the activity level of young children and were
taken aback when Peter took all three out for a walk in the bitter
cold. Later when we had our own kids, we understood. Peter
had by then developed a passion for gourmet living, or more
accurately a combination of gourmet and gourmand.

In the years that followed we would meet mostly in
London when I was passing through. Many times we went
down to Berwick St John, a small village in Wiltshire where
Peter and Sylvia had a cottage. Peter always tried to arrange his
crowded schedule in London, Paris and Genoa so as to spend
his weekends there. He loved to go running and kept very fit.
That was the place where he could turn off, relax and hone his
cooking skills. We sometimes talked about engineering and

Peter and Sylvia
on their wedding
day, London
1961.

11

physics, my profession, and found that both of us were stronger on ideas than on the technical calculations.

Peter was always so healthy and full of life that the brain tumour came as a great shock to all and especially to him. The combination of a deadly prognosis and great restrictions on his sight were hard blows, at a time when he was in his fifties and his professional life was flourishing. But he did not withdraw and feel bitter about his cruel fate. He set about making the most of his remaining time. He produced the book *An Engineer Imagines* articulating his philosophy about the interaction of engineers and architects and lobbying for a more equal and productive relationship. The book is fascinating, even for someone like me from outside the profession, and a remarkable achievement under the circumstances.

Even more remarkable to my mind was his performance at the award ceremony for the RIBA Gold Medal just a few months before he died. First, his close colleagues, Renzo Piano and

Peter and Sylvia
with daughter
Julia on her
wedding day,
Gourgoubès
1992.

Richard Rogers, introduced him and then he spoke. He had no notes and anyway he could not read. He wore a hat to cover up the mess that the radiation treatment made of his full head of hair. He knew that he was dying and was saying goodbye forever. The large audience of distinguished engineers and architects, family and friends, knew that too. Yet he did not become in any way emotional or sentimental, but delivered an eloquent speech on the relationship between architects and engineers. His message was that engineers should not be the ones to frustrate the best ideas of the architects but that the two should work together and explore the possibilities opened by advances in materials to create new and soaring structures. Afterwards when I asked him how he pulled it off, he just answered that it is easy when you know what message you want to deliver!

Later in the summer of 1992, Sylvia and he organized a party over several days at Gourgoubès in the Languedoc for the wedding of their eldest daughter, Julia. A big happy party for family and friends was how he chose to say goodbye.

2

# Peter Rice, engineer

Jack Zunz

**W**hen I was asked to make a contribution to this publication on the life and work of Peter Rice, I did not want to repeat what I said and wrote about him after his untimely death. His personal qualities, his exceptional talents, have been, and will continue to be, a subject for celebration and reflection. Instead, and in some ways in keeping with the title of this book, I want to revisit the route that took Peter to the very summit of his profession; a route, which in hindsight though quite logical, was nevertheless long, yet straight and not without elements of serendipity.

I first met Peter in the latter part of 1961, when I was assembling Arup's team to design and construct the roof for Sydney Opera House. Peter was part of a small team that had been engaged in carrying out model tests and geometric studies. A change in direction led to some of the team deciding that they had had enough. I wanted Peter to stay and play his part in what increasingly appeared to be an exciting, if partly uncharted, journey. Peter, then a comparatively inexperienced young graduate and ever thoughtful, wanted time to deliberate and take stock before deciding whether or not he wanted to carry on. After a week, he came back stating that he wanted to continue working on the project, but needed my assurance he would be sent to Sydney to be part of the team on site supervising construction. I told him that I would make every effort to fulfill his wish. This is when my association with Peter started.

Even with hindsight it is difficult to imagine that this very bright, sensitive and thoughtful engineer would become one of the most talented designers of engineering structures of his generation. He did not appear to have any special concern for the design of structures. I cannot remember him attending any meetings with Jørn Utzon or his co-workers. His main interest was in the *analysis* of structures, and he was exceptionally good at it. He was one of the first to harness electronic computers to solve engineering problems, computers that by current standards were antediluvian. Despite recurring electricity failures he coaxed from cupboards full of thermionic valves reams of punched tape that he read accurately and assiduously. He worked on the analysis of parts of the main roof and was central to our being able to start producing some drawings from which the roof structure could actually be built. Peter had now acquired greater confidence in his abilities not only to analyze complex structures, but also to ensure that the results of these analyses were properly translated into workable details ready for construction.

When we reached the stage where drawings for construction were emerging we spoke about moving him to Sydney to play his part on site in a supervisory role, as we had agreed. An experienced and very capable Resident Engineer had guided the project to the stage where construction of the roof could commence. I considered it to be necessary to have engineers on site who were familiar with the roof analysis and there was no one better than Peter who had detailed knowledge of the predicted behaviour of this rather unusual structure. Peter was also keen to play his part in its realization. It was now 1963 and he and his family moved to Sydney.

Peter Rice and
Dr Lionel
Geoffrey Booth
with drawing
of Sydney Opera
House (Jørn
Utzon), c.1960.

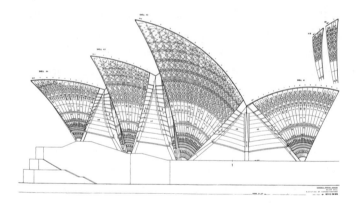

Elevation of
superstructure of
Sydney Opera
House, Drawing
by Ove Arup and
Partners (Yuzo
Mikami), 1964.

Sydney Opera
House under
construction,
c.1965.

On the site at Bennelong Point, Peter's contribution proved to be immense. He used his formidable intellect to help solve seemingly intractable problems in rectifying unpredicted deformations during erection. He wrote computer programmes that enabled the contractor to predict accurate positioning of the structural elements. He also experienced the real problems that can only be learnt on site, actually being part of the construction process. He learnt to develop the art of the possible, the manner in which one can open up the boundaries of accepted practice. Above all, he came into contact with Jørn Utzon.

Utzon was persuasively lyrical when speaking about architecture, particularly his own. When walking around the site with the resident staff, he spoke about his vision of colour, light and texture in a way that made an indelible impression on Peter. He described his aims and objectives in architecture at an intellectual level that matched Peter's own. I believe that listening to Utzon articulating in particular his visual objective, seeds were planted that awakened Peter's nascent interest in design for concepts of structure in architecture, which was to come to such spectacular fruition some years later.

This later passion for design, however, was still dormant. After three years in Sydney, and when the construction of the roof was well advanced, he wrote to me asking to have a year away from practice and become a visiting scholar at Cornell University. In his letter he said, *inter alia*, 'I would like to study the application of pure mathematics to engineering problems. I think that a more thorough understanding of the nature of the equations used to solve structural problems in design could lead to a better conditioned solution and ultimately to a better choice of structural components.'

In many ways this was typical Peter. There was no wish to add letters to his name. He was simply seeking knowledge to enable him to find better and possibly new solutions to the problems he might face.

Peter returned to Arup in London in 1968. He had gained confidence and maturity. His superb analytical skills were harnessed to the full in working on fabric and other lightweight structures with Frei Otto. The real flowering of Peter's talents,

Positioning of structural element, Sydney Opera House, c.1965.

however, became evident when he met Renzo Piano and Richard Rogers during the design for the international competition of what was subsequently called Centre Pompidou.

Like Sydney Opera House, the choice of the winning design raised eyebrows. Piano and Rogers' scheme was the stuff of avant-garde schools of architecture influenced by state-of-the-art prophets like 'Archigram'. Now these ideas had to be coaxed into reality, there was no scope for fudging obvious problems. What is more, the building was to be erected in the centre of one of the most culturally sensitive cities in the world, Paris.

Peter Rice, Renzo Piano and Richard Rogers turned out to be kindred spirits. While Peter then (and later) deferred to architects where their expertise was obvious and seminal, he had now established the confidence to use his exceptional talents to complement rather than to defer to those architects with whom he was working. Not only did he explore the use of novel ways in assembling and configuring structures and the materials from which they were made, but also directed his formidable analytical capabilities in helping his architectural colleagues to explore the problems they were trying to solve in the first place. He became a master of his craft and had acquired the confidence to practise it.

It could be said that the concept, application and subsequent successful functioning of the now legendary gerberettes proved to be a nodal point in Peter's career. Here was Peter, probably inspired by the exuberance of Victorian engineering, resurrecting a material that had fallen into disuse in contemporary structural engineering, revisiting concepts in the use of this material, which others have followed. The application of the gerberettes and other elements in cast steel were also a testament to his clarity of thought. It enabled him to articulate structures in a comprehensible manner that was to be a hallmark of much of his work. He established a resonant relationship with his architectural colleagues, which not only made this structural expression possible but also helped those architects to gain insights into new possibilities in the work on which they were engaged.

Post Centre Pompidou he was more and more in demand. Many of the great and the good in the international architectural galaxy sought out his talents. He now had the confidence to break fresh ground when appropriate. His self-belief flourished, underpinned by clarity of thought, analytical strengths, increasing knowledge and understanding of materials and above all increasing interest and understanding of the totality of design. Peter had become a star, but he also understood the real essence of teamwork and was never afraid to give generous credit to those who merited it.

Peter's road to stardom had been long, but his light shone all the brighter for that. His talents had developed with a strong intellectual spine allied to a warm personality. His relationships with collaborators, particularly some of the world's great architects, were not only developed on the grounds of his professional talents, but also through enjoyable personal encounters. His relationships with both Renzo Piano and Richard Rogers probably remained the strongest. It was forged in the heat of creating Centre Pompidou and arguably resulted in a surge of creativity that may well have been the launch-pad of the subsequent success all three have enjoyed.

In the Anglo-Saxon world the title, the word, 'engineer' has many connotations. It is a truism that the public at large has little understanding and awareness of the role of the engineer in the design and construction of buildings. Peter found that in the light of his manifestly mammoth contribution to the projects on which he was engaged, this lack of understanding resulted in offers of new titles, 'architectural engineer' or even 'architect'. Peter would have none of it. In the address he gave to the RIBA on being awarded its Gold Medal, he said, 'I'm an engineer pure and simple.' One can only speculate what additional contribution he might have made to engineering had he not been struck down so cruelly at the height of his powers.

The Rice family had a house where Peter's widow Sylvia still lives, in a small Wiltshire village, Berwick St John. Peter's final resting place is in the graveyard adjacent to the church. There a simple headstone reads:

PETER RICE

ENGINEER

Future Systems Museum of the Moving Image (MOMI) Tent interior, London 1991.

Future Systems MOMI Tent interior detail.

# Amanda Levete

I MET PETER in 1984 when I was starting out as an architect, it was my first day working at Richard Rogers. I obviously knew of Peter's work, I hugely admired the structure of Centre Pompidou and the significance of the building on every level – I was in awe of him. On that first day I asked him some very naïve questions but he was patient, warm and never patronizing. I continued to work with Peter right up until his death. Our only built work together was the MOMI Tent that Jan Kaplický and I did at Future Systems. It was a small, low cost project for a demountable building but Peter didn't care about scale or the number of cubic metres of concrete you poured, he was interested in ideas. We wanted to design an impossibly fragile structure – he likened it to fishing rod technology. Picking up a Tipp-Ex bottle on his desk he promised the diameter of the fibreglass rods spanning 10 metres would be no bigger than that.

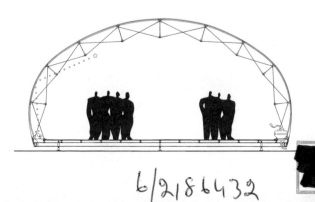

Section drawing, MOMI Tent.

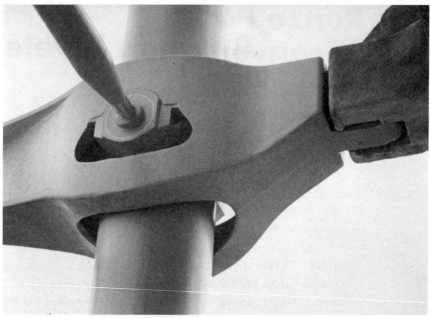

22

Gerberette and column, Centre Pompidou, Paris 1974.

3

# Renzo Piano
# in conversation

Kevin Barry & Jennifer Greitschus

n a room named the *jardin d'hiver*, lit from above, at the back of his Paris studio, Renzo Piano remembers Peter Rice. The studio space on rue des Archives is lively and open. It is airy but not large. Between Paris and his office in Genoa approximately 130 people work together in the Renzo Piano Building Workshop. He has chosen to limit the physical size of the office so as to keep the practice relatively small and intimate, so that everyone knows each other well. The memory of Peter Rice, he feels, is all around him, and especially next door in the *atelier* where colleagues are at work cutting materials and modelling pieces.

'At Beaubourg in the early 1970s,' recalls Renzo Piano, 'we were all young, bad-boy humanists: Peter Rice, Richard Rogers, Ted Happold. We wanted to mix together architecture, beauty, structure, and physics. When we met for the Beaubourg competition, in 1971, we were in our thirties. In Paris at that time practice was based on the tradition of the Beaux-Arts architects who made sketches and left it to others to see to the construction. We arrived in a completely different spirit. For us architecture and construction must come together: beauty, rebellion and invention, all together. Our purpose was to distance ourselves from formulas, in order to make a building that would be good for culture: flexible, able to change over the centuries. One day, some months into this struggle, Ove Arup arrived in Paris and he affirmed our methods. He was most understanding. At that moment we became at one with Ove. The legend became physical. He had defended us. We were also lucky because in January 1972 another great man, Robert Bordaz, was named president of the public establishment of the Centre Beaubourg with responsibility for its construction, and he supported us. We needed these senior figures. When you are thirty-five or thirty-six years old, you can find yourself in trouble: you may know what is right but you cannot prove it. We needed Ove Arup and we needed Robert Bordaz, both older men, to provide their backing; giving us a sense of security, assuring us that when we insisted they would be there to protect us, they were our guardian angels.'

During the early 1970s, as Plateau Beaubourg took shape as the Centre Pompidou, Renzo Piano and Peter Rice discovered that they had much in common. Both of their wives were soon to give birth and the two men shared the suspense of waiting. In Renzo Piano's phrase, they discovered an 'affinity with one another'.

'When Peter Rice and I worked together, it was impossible sometimes to know from our conversations who was the engineer and who was the architect. It was a continuous game of ping-pong between us. I had been born into the world of building. My father was a builder. I grew up never making a difference between shape and construction. For that reason working closely with Peter came easily to me. I grew up on building sites. The site was pure magic; even the most modest site was magic. Someone has said that at that age you have discovered the essence of your life and I think that is probably true.

'Peter liked to play games, guessing-games. He would guess what time it was: he never wore a watch. To guess the time is to have a better sense of the value of time passing.

Rooftop terrace, Centre Pompidou.

View from north-east, Centre Pompidou.

He would estimate at a glance the volume of a structure, of a column, of a mass. We would compete in this game. We were both good at it, but he was better than me. Our understanding of structure was instinctive and completely physical. Each of us invaded the other's field. Peter would speak about the expression of the building and its emotion, its light, and its lightness. Lightness is a funny game: fighting against the force of gravity. Playing these games together was fantastic, magical. We did not first conceive a form and then make it functional. Rather the structure was from the beginning, both beautiful and good. In some cultures the word beauty does not exist without reference to goodness: for us, an engineer and an architect working together, the beauty and goodness of a building were one and the same. For this reason we both admired Jean Prouvé: no one can say if he was an architect or an engineer. It is not being moralistic to declare that today architecture seems at moments a lost art because it has become formal: without beauty and goodness coming together in built structures.

'It was in a little office on Aybrook Street, London, that we started the work on Beaubourg and we immediately understood that we saw things in the same spirit: a building made of pieces that come together. Richard Rogers was very keen to say, and he was right to say it, that a building for culture must be able to change continuously. We sketched it out, and it was a machine, a human machine. We would talk of the beauty of the bicycle, for example, or of the umbrella. There are certain things that are beautiful by definition because everyone understands so immediately how they work. In reality the gerberette and beam create a sense of balance that is self-expressing, giving a special life to the structure. That was Peter's work. And when something like that comes your way, you grasp it. When Mr Honda came from Japan to visit us on the site, he said (speaking through a translator) that it was a beautiful building. We asked the translator why. And the reply came: because it is like a motorbike. Like a Honda! For us that had been part of the plan: to make a building for culture that looked like a machine, that was the opposite of monumentality and intimidation, of marble buildings. When people declared

Finishing surface of roof leaf, Menil Collection museum.

that Centre Pompidou looked like a refinery or like a factory we were very pleased to say yes, that is exactly what we wanted.'

After the completion of the Centre Pompidou, in 1977, the architect and the engineer set up together the Atelier Piano and Rice. The partnership created several projects during the four years of its existence: the *Il Rigo* Quarter, Corciano, Perugia, 1978–82; the Fiat VSS experimental car, 1978–80; the Otranto Urban Regeneration Workshop, 1979; the Burano Island Regeneration Workshop, Venice, 1980. The partnership was dissolved in 1981. 'We both came to decide that it was not a good idea. An engineer needs a wider range of opportunities. An architect needs from time to time to work with other engineers. The spirit of our working together was more important than giving it an organizational structure. And we ceased the organizational partnership while continuing to collaborate on many projects. After Peter's death I have continued to work with Ove Arup, because so many people there have a philosophy akin to his printed under their skin. These people are happy to move between different fields: there is a DNA that remains, not always perhaps, but it is still there.'

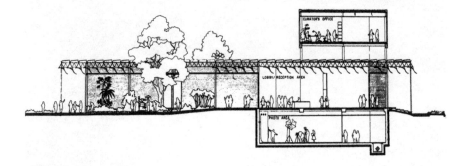

The Irish engineer Peter Rice grew up in Dundalk, Renzo Piano in Genoa, and Richard Rogers in Florence. At Beaubourg they communicated with each other across different languages. 'With Richard Rogers I spoke Italian, because Richard was born and grew up in Italy. But with Peter we used to speak to each other in French for the simple reason that it was neither English nor Italian. So we both spoke slowly: for both of us it was an intermediary. He was Irish, I was Italian, and we loved mixing things together. He was a humanist. He loved art, loved working with artists, loved music, wine, food, and horses as well. He was a man of many interests, and an Italian like me is also always mixing things together: technology, arts and cities.

'I remember one evening in Paris we went out for a meal together. We were at the time designing the Menil Collection museum and struggling with how to fabricate those "leaf" elements of the roof that had to do two very demanding things: to hold in place a roof spanning more than 12 metres, and to bring natural light inside from above. I was telling Peter a story about Pier Luigi Nervi, the Italian engineer, who had made a ferro-cement boat. Suddenly, Peter proposed that we use ferro-cement for the roof elements at Menil. I love building boats, and some years before I had already made my boat in ferro-

Elevated superstructure, Menil Collection museum (Renzo Piano), Houston 1981.

Exterior, Menil Collection museum.

cement. Peter helped me with the sketches. Ferro-cement is a funny combination of steel and concrete. The steel is very dense: a fine mesh. The conversation over dinner gave us a solution to the Menil Collection museum. Being Irish and Italian, we were happy to share the enjoyment we took in things.

'His special legacy for me is his sense of the integrity of a building as its most important value. It is not about how a building looks, but what it is. He had a quick mental understanding of the way a building works and he never forgot that a building must mix the architectural and the social; that it must provide a good shelter. He had a constant desire: to play against gravity. This is why we both loved Alexander Calder: a grown-up boy playing all the time with balance. Conversations with Peter were always playful and changed every few minutes. They were never just about architecture or construction but always moved around to music, horses, football, soccer, art, and artists. Peter Rice remains around me where I work with my colleagues. To be here in the office or to be next door in the workshop is to be among traces of Peter Rice – many, many traces.'

Menil Collection
museum interior.

Menil Collection
museum interior.

Menil Collection museum interior.

Fine-tuning the light, Menil Collection museum.

# 4

# Peter Rice, lighting engineer

Andy Sedgwick

Perhaps surprisingly, a number of Peter Rice's projects have no relation to structural engineering at all. I was lucky in my early career to benefit from Peter's developing interest in light, and natural light in particular.

The Arup group I joined in London in 1983 was led by Tom Barker and Peter Rice. Tom was a mechanical engineer and led the building services team, and Peter led the structural engineers. It was probably the most dynamic and innovative building engineering team Arup has ever had: the group had its roots in Centre Pompidou, when Peter and Tom worked together in Arup's project office in Paris. When I joined, the majority of the group was busy in the thick of production design for Lloyds of London, but Peter and Tom found time to progress a number of other important projects, including the Menil Collection in Houston and the IBM Travelling Pavilion, both with Renzo Piano Building Workshop. Natural light was a key factor in these projects. At Menil, daylight is the prime illuminant of the gallery walls – largely by reflection and diffusion between the ferro-cement leaves that form part of the roof structure – direct Texas sun is far too bright for the display of works of art. In a similar way, daylight entry through the clear polycarbonate skin of the Travelling Pavilion building needed moderation to allow effective viewing of the many computer screens that comprised much of the exhibition.

I joined Arup as an electrical engineer, but on my first day I found on my desk the 606-page 'bible' on natural light: *Daylighting* by Hopkinson, Petherbridge and Longmore. Tom had decided Arup needed a daylighting specialist. I developed some Fortran programmes to calculate how natural light levels would vary in the Travelling Pavilion for each of the twenty different European cities it would visit for a month. Depending on the time of year, the local climate and the planned orientation of the Pavilion, a specific arrangement of opaque and diffusing pyramidal inserts was derived for each site.

The roof system for Menil was already designed – the daylighting had been fine-tuned through a series of scale models and full-scale prototypes. I picked up some computer graphic software that Tristram Carfrae had written, and used it to visualize test data from some of the scale-model testing. The age of computer simulation of lighting effects was beginning.

Peter was invited by I.M. Pei to work with him on the Grand Projet to redevelop the Louvre in Paris during the mid-1980s. Rice Francis Ritchie consulted on the construction phase of the Pyramide du Louvre, and Peter was asked to work with Pei on filigree glazed roofs to enclose three courtyards in the Richelieu wing of the Palais du Louvre: Cour Khorsabad, Cour Puget and Cour Marly. The wing had previously been the Finance Ministry, and the interior spaces were being converted to house applied and decorative arts on the first floor, and the Musée du Louvre's collection of German, Dutch and Flemish paintings on the second floor. After an early meeting on the courtyard roofs Peter came to find me back in London and asked if I thought we could design daylighting systems for all of the top floor painting galleries in Richelieu: thirty-nine galleries in all, with thirteen unique solutions. He said, 'If we

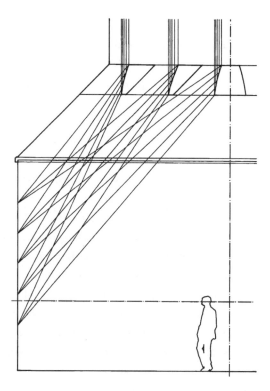

Geometrical study
to determine
form of plaster
blades for
daylight system,
Richelieu Wing,
Louvre 1985.

pull this off we'll have an instant pedigree in museum lighting'
– he didn't need to tell me what the consequences would be if
we got it wrong.

Many historic gallery spaces at the Louvre – such as the
Grande Gallerie – are generously top-lit by rooflights with
diffuse laylights beneath. Electric lighting is hidden, but equally
there is no direct view of the sky. Pei wanted the new painting
galleries in the Richelieu Wing to have a similar atmosphere
– with visitors experiencing the works under daylight alone for
most of the year – but he also wanted to go one step further and
be able to glimpse the sky from within the galleries.

Peter and I were joined by Andrew McDowell, one of
the first pure mathematicians employed by Arup. Together we
developed our finite element, radiosity exchange software to
model the entry and flow of natural light within the gallery
spaces. The computational method was too slow – to model
each gallery and its daylighting system and calculate the light

flows took a week every time we changed something – and Pei's team kept a rapid pace. So instead we derived some geometric methods that could be used by Yann Weymouth and Andrzej Gorczynski in Pei's team to generate the forms of the plaster blades that direct daylight towards the walls, and form the visual ceiling of each gallery.

The use of moving parts to respond to the variation of natural light levels was quickly ruled out – like many institutions the Louvre had an aversion to anything that required maintenance. Each gallery room therefore has a fixed and passive daylight system. This means that light levels on the paintings vary through each day and through the year. Instead of designing for fixed light levels set by the curators, as happens with electric light, an alternative approach based on 'illumination exposure' is needed. The integral of light over time is managed – to ensure that artworks receive an acceptable dose of light each year. Gaining the curators acceptance of this approach was a crucial step in the design process. Peter's role was as 'understander and explainer' – he would grill me on every aspect and angle of an issue, ask me all the difficult questions, before he was ready to present the work himself to a crowded hall at the Louvre.

We made some big mistakes. I took to Paris a scale model of one gallery, about the size of a packing crate, and we viewed it with Pei and his team on a fine day in the Tuileries Gardens. We took it in turns to put our heads under a black cloak and peer into the model: with no time for adaption from the high outdoor light levels the inner surfaces of the model looked incredibly dingy – even though the daylight levels were correct. It felt more like a cave than an art gallery. We learnt our lesson, and when a full scale mockup was created one year later we included an antechamber where people waited for two minutes for their eyes to adjust before entering the main room.

Peter's last project at the Louvre, the Pyramide Inversée, is both a remarkable piece of structure and an engaging optic device. The tensegrity net of rods and cables supports four planes of low-iron glass that form the pyramid. Standing at the junction of two underground malls, the planes of glass act as a periscope, giving an unexpected reflection of the sky deep below ground.

Natural light distributed by fixed plaster blades beneath pitched skylights, Rubens Gallery, Richelieu Wing, Louvre 1985.

Typical Richelieu Wing top-lit gallery with cruciform ceiling.

Richelieu skylights: sun-blocking screens above light-directing plaster blades.

Full-Moon Theatre
grid-shell reflector design,
May 1991.

38

I've often wondered why it was that Peter developed such a passionate interest in the physics and manipulation of daylight – we never had that discussion explicitly. Superficially it's a straightforward architectural discipline – you position glazed holes in the envelope of a building, and daylight will enter. But daylight varies continuously – with the time of year, the time of day and with cloud cover to name the most obvious variables, so the temporal availability and spatial distribution of daylight are complex to describe and always in motion. The physics of optics and the mathematics of the statistical presentation of daylight parameters probably appealed to Peter, but of course the human experience of light is elemental and mediated by the eye/brain instrument. It's possible to talk about light in terms of physics and mathematics, but there's plenty of room for philosophy and poetry too.

The Full-Moon Theatre project began, as did many others, with long evening discussions in Peter's office over-looking Fitzroy Square. Humbert Camerlo, an opera director and a longstanding friend of Peter's, lived near Montpellier in the south of France on an ancient estate called Gourgoubès. Humbert and Peter conceived the idea of a small experimental theatre, out amongst the olive groves, where the only light source for performances would be the light of the full moon. We soon realized that large areas of light collectors would be

Full-Moon
Theatre grid-shell
reflectors,
June 1991.

needed to magnify the moonlight, which even on a cloudless night at full moon is only 1/500,000<sup>th</sup> of the intensity of sunlight.

With a near zero budget, high-tech solutions were out of the question, and we looked for a craft-based approach that could be constructed by masons and carpenters in the middle of the French countryside. In the spring of 1991 we designed the geometry of a stone amphitheatre that faced the locus of the summer full moon, and as the May full moon approached we rushed to produce designs for the first moonlight concentrators. We used cutting pattern programmes that Peter had used for tensile fabric structures to derive the coordinates of plywood panels and timber laths that were fed in to a fax machine for transmission to Gourgoubès. When assembled these timber gridshells took parabolic forms, with the stage at the focus point. These forms were then lined with silvered mylar sheeting and mounted on steel gimbal frames to create mobile, aimable reflectors. The experimental performances could begin.

Peter was particularly interested in all the physical properties of moonlight – if we could harness concentrated moonlight, could it have other uses beyond performance: scientific, medical, artistic? Are there colours or industrial processes that are only possible under moonlight? We came down with a bump when we realized that moonlight is only sunlight, reflected from the dark grey, slightly yellow surface lunar surface. But that reflection does remove nearly all the infra-red and ultraviolet parts of the spectrum – moonlight is very close to a 'pure visible light'.

The story of the conception and first years of the Full-Moon Theatre is beautifully told in one of the last chapters of Peter's book, *An Engineer Imagines*. As the first incarnation of the theatre at Gourgoubès was completed in the summer of 1991, Peter was again 'understander and explainer': the TV executives who visited in August were a little underwhelmed by the artisanal nature of the undertaking: was this the same Peter Rice who manipulated steel and glass with such precision in Paris? Peter would describe, as he does in the book, that he felt that what was 'essential in the Full-Moon Theatre, and in the Gourgoubès project generally, is that everything that happens there is rooted in the place and comes from the hands of people who live and work there' – and that the spiritual, and experiential aspects of the project were more important than the technology and its effects.

Twenty years later experimentation at Gourgoubès remains a challenge – there have been many generations of moonlight collectors since our earliest trials with Peter. Those of us who have been involved count our blessings that we shared in a unique and humanistic experiment. And I'm grateful for the education in daylight that I received through these and other projects from Tom Barker, Renzo Piano, and Peter Rice.

Overview of Full-Moon Theatre seen from the stage. (Humbert Camerlo), Gourgoubès 1992.

Overview of Full-Moon Theatre, Gourgoubès, December 2007.

Passerelle Simone de Beauvoir, detail of lens with steel stamens delimiting tripartite volume (Dietmar Feichtinger), Paris 2006.

Barge with central pectinate lens of the Seine passerelle approaching the Pont Neuf, Paris 30 November 2005.

# Henry Bardsley

THERE ARE spoken traces, built traces, and mathematical traces.

A built trace is the passerelle across the Seine on the axis of the Bibliothèque Nationale, a project designed in 1998. The bridge differentiates compression and tension. It uses thick steel tension bars to control deflections in a slender structure. The double structure at the support creates a scissor point, stabilized with barettes down to the limestone horizon. Both structures are related to heroic transport of large components; the trusses of Beaubourg travelled by rail and road from the Ruhr; the lens of the Seine bridge came by dynamic river barge from the mid Rhine, paused at Vissingen, rounded Cap Gris Nez, arriving through the Seine locks. Both the footbridge and the Centre Pompidou explore the limits of toughness of thick materials, and become as such scale-related. In both projects the castings were initially outside specification. However in the bridge the details contrast, either solecistic, drawn as forgings made as castings, or uncelebrated. But also a denial, a scheme successful in competition, by differentiation with the unsuccessful hoop tied bridge scheme across the Seine at Austerlitz.

Peter's mathematical traces were marked by the laborious manual work on the spherical geometries of Sydney. His dialogue with Alistair Day's software defined much of his work in structures. One of his contributions to the Cour Marly of the Louvre was based on cylinders and repetitivity. But how would he have expressed himself, twenty years on, with the geometrical software tools we have today?

Peter's spoken traces were related to the linguistic tunnel between London and Paris. Phrases and interests in London sprouted into a different life in Paris. Independence of scale of a light model. The framing. Emptiness of the center. Mastership of scale by mathematics. Dislike of sugar. Concern for fire safety. Two-week work cycle.

My exemplary trace is still his capacity to confront adversity, not only to design at the vanguard, but to guide a project through difficult straits. The most significant trace is the absence of trace. As Viking mariners traversed the traceless oceans, guided by magnetic needle fragments, Peter would develop his project from their internal coherence, with little reference to examples.

**43**

Lightweight steel-mesh stairs within triple height open-plan section of Richard Rogers' terrace house, London.

5

# Richard Rogers
# in conversation

Jonathan Glancey

At home in Chelsea, Richard Rogers is reminded of Peter Rice every day. The Irish engineer designed the long, bounding flights of lightweight steel-mesh stairs that stretch effortlessly from floor to floor of the triple height open-plan section of the architect's radically remodelled London terrace house. The bounce built into the structure of the stairs makes them exceptionally easy, and enjoyable, to run up and down; they are ingenious, playful and very friendly. 'Like Peter,' says Rogers.

'Peter was a delight to work with. He had an innate sense of design, but was never presumptuous. He kept his cool under pressure. He certainly didn't seek fame or money. He lived modestly, but he lived to the full; he had a great sense of fun and loved wine, women and song!' He was a great family man and they were all very close, his wife Sylvia, his son Kieran who worked with Peter at RFR in Paris – he's the president of the group now – his daughters Nemone, Heidi, Julia and Nicki. They were all a part of our lives; Peter was wonderful at connecting people.

'I see him as an artist, a poet, a sculptor engineer or engineer sculptor, a humanist, a Brunelleschi of recent times. He crossed boundaries, stimulated all our imaginations and was always optimistic. He came to our RRP [Richard Rogers Partnership] Monday morning design meetings, and I'd say that Peter was involved in 90 per cent of our projects until he died. He was a huge influence on how we thought and what we built over twenty years.'

Along with a team of spirited young architects and equally young and inventive fellow engineers, Peter Rice was one of the three key designers, along with Richard Rogers and Renzo Piano, of the Centre Pompidou, the startling and brilliant Parisian project that made their names and reputations both collectively and individually.

'Peter transformed the competition entry for Pompidou from a design that was in some ways too mechanistic into one that was humanistic. He had a natural sense of scale and proportion. He was an artist and a fine mathematician. He softened the whole look of the building through the way he reconfigured the structure. There's a lot of handcraft in the building, which might surprise many people, and that's one of Peter's great contributions. The cast-steel gerberettes that allowed us to have a deep, free floor space by carrying the weight of the floors to the outside of the building in a sequence of light tubes instead of heavy steel columns brought a light and grace to the final structure, but they were also fettled by hand.

'Peter was thrilled when he came across an old Parisian lady stroking the cast steel and telling him how lovely the texture was. Peter helped us to create what we like to think of as architecture as a "soft machine"; because of his contribution, "hi-tech" was never as mechanistic as it might have been.

'Of course, the funny thing looking back is that, to begin with, I hadn't been at all keen on the project. It had come from Ted Happold [the Ove Arup and Partners engineer whose Structures 3 team within the firm specializing in the design of lightweight structures included the young Peter Rice]. Ted saw the notice calling for entries to the Pompidou competition, and wrote off for details. I've always said, "It was all Ted's idea!" I didn't want to work for a right-wing President, or a centralized museum for a highly centralized regime. But Ted, Renzo and others persuaded me to give it a go, and we – the "bad boys" as Renzo called us – won.

'We thought of our entry as the "British Museum crossed with Times Square". The idea was influenced by Cedric Price and Joan Littlewood's Fun Palace [1961], by Archigram's Plug In City [1961] and by [the writings of] Reyner Banham. Ted had recommended Renzo and me as architects to work with Arup on the competition and this brought us in touch with Peter, who really came into his own once we began work together in Paris on the commissioned project.

'One of the things we had to adapt to very quickly was the fact that the budget we had assumed we were working to was double the real figure. So we had to cut back on ideas like moving floors that rose up and down the building. We also had to reduce its height when new fire regulations – invented for Pompidou as it was a new type of building – were agreed. The authorities settled on a maximum roof height of 28 metres, but in our competition design we were over 40 metres! But, as we cut back, and as the building became lower and denser, this gave Peter the opportunity to show how brilliant he was as a designer and as an engineer.'

47

The young team reduced the bulk, weight, height and mechanical complexity of the competition design and, as it did so, a highly distinctive architecture began to emerge. Not for nothing was the *Architectural Review* to draw a distinction in the years following the completion of the Centre Pompidou between what it perceived as the modern 'Gothic' work of the Richard Rogers Partnership and the 'Classical' nature of that of Foster and Partners. This made a certain sense: whereas the Foster office produced beautifully sleek machine-like 'hi-tech' buildings such as the Willis Faber headquarters in Ipswich and the Sainsbury Centre for Visual Arts for the University of East Anglia at Norwich, the highly expressive designs of RRP, characterized by Peter Rice's lightweight suspended roof structures, and especially perhaps the gerberettes of Pompidou, evoked the articulated massing and, in the case of the latter, even the flying buttresses of the most adventurous medieval cathedrals.

'The gerberettes were a brilliant idea. Peter gave every credit to Lennart Grut [very young then; a director of Rogers, Stirk and Harbour today] and Johnny Stanton, another very young guy [currently Professor of Structural Engineering and Mechanics at the University of Washington] for the idea. The idea of using cast steel in modern buildings was largely unheard of, although Kenzo Tange had used it and Frei Otto was using it in the roof of the Olympic Stadium [1972 Olympic Games], under construction in Munich. Peter went to see that. We all admired Frei Otto. In fact, we had tried to work with him before Pompidou with a proposal we made with Wolff Olins [the design consultancy] for a new grandstand for Chelsea [Football Club]. That came to nothing, but it was Frei Otto who put us in touch with Ted and Arup, and so to Peter.'

Although cast steel was rarely a structural feature of modern architecture – if casting is flawed, cracks can appear at unexpected moments – it was used and still is, in dams, power stations, turbochargers and turbines driving the world's fastest and most up-to-date ships. When impeccably cast, steel components are strong, highly effective and also rather beautiful.

Rice also looked long and hard at the Grand Palais, the voluptuous, yet lightweight glass-and-steel Parisian exhibition hall built for the 1900 World Fair. 'Peter engineered – designed – lightness and humanity into Pompidou. It was something he was to do with many of our projects, and, of course, also for Renzo, Norman [Foster], Ian Ritchie, Paul Andreu, Kenzo Tange and others. Not that it was plain sailing. When the first gerberette was 'cooked', it cracked. We panicked! If they hadn't worked, we'd have had to redesign the entire structure! Again, Peter solved the problem; it was something to do with exactly how long the castings were allowed to cool. It was a distinctly worrying moment; we were pushing the boundaries and couldn't afford, in any way, to get things wrong.'

The expressive, increasingly filigree roof structures Rice devised and designed with the Rogers team led to buildings that no matter how rudimentarily functional exhibited something of the grace, invention and playfulness of both the Grand Palais and Centre Pompidou. A good example is the Fleetguard factory

Fleetguard factory
(Richard Rogers
& Partners),
Quimper.

[1978–81] outside Quimper in Brittany. Built for a division of
the Cummins Engine Company for the manufacture of engine
filters, the brief required a maximum of clear covered space and
a building that could be readily extended. Rice's lightweight
tensile roof structure, picked out in eye-catching red paint,
not only fulfilled the demands of the brief, but gave shape
to what was essentially little more than a glorified warehouse
that, nevertheless, editors of architectural magazines clamoured
to publish images of. Just as the great timber tithe barns of
medieval England are the stuff of compelling architectural and
structural sorcery, so, too, is the Fleetguard factory.

'Peter never wanted to standardize structures,' says Rogers.
'Each new project was to be looked at afresh, to produce the
most elegant as well as the most efficient design. This is under-
standable given not only Rice's inherent love of natural as
well as man-made beauty, but also because he had wanted to
be an aeronautical engineer before he switched to structural
engineering and, perhaps, because his first major project
with Arup was the daring roof, or roofscape, of Jørn Utzon's
sensational Sydney Opera House.

'One of the most beautiful roofs he designed was for our original scheme for Terminal 5 [Heathrow Airport]. Peter imagined it as an elongated wave, and only he could have engineered it. But, as constraints emerged, we had to rework the design on a much smaller site, and build up rather than horizontally. So we never got Peter's wave, which I still think is a shame.

'Before working with Peter, we existed in a world of I-beams and the kind of steelwork that would have made the walls of Pompidou look heavy; we were looking for transparency, the idea of a cultural centre that was truly open to everyone with nothing to hide from the public. With standard steel components, we couldn't have got this.'

Although Rogers was particularly keen on developing a transparent and open-ended architecture in steel and glass, this was not always possible. In fact, one of RRP's most celebrated designs, the Lloyds of London Building [1978–86] is, for all its pewter-like steel cladding, a concrete structure. 'It wasn't a material I felt happy using,' says Rogers. 'It seemed heavy and bulky, but we had no choice because fire regulations insisted on it. Peter showed how we could explore concrete and create a structure that was as light as the material is heavy. He went on, with Renzo, to show how even stone construction has new possibilities; so, I needn't have been so hung up on steel!'

As well as drawing attention to the modern Gothic nature of Rogers' designs of the 1980s, the *Architectural Review* highlighted the fact that despite their many references to machines and machine technology, these 'hi-tech' buildings represented a fresh flowering of craft in architecture. A tendency to reject standardized componentry in favour of materials like cast steel, and for the need to employ teams of highly skilled construction workers to realize these radical new structures, did indeed lead to the flourishing of a way of working that the Modern Movement had seemed to have vanquished.

'Peter brought a humanity and poetry to contemporary architecture,' says Richard Rogers. 'There are a number of great engineers out there today, but we've never been able to find another Peter Rice. There were, of course, Ove Arup himself and Jack Zunz at Arup both of whom were brilliant, humanistic engineers; they loved Peter and what he was doing and gave him all the slack he needed to work both within and without the firm to ensure he was happy and creative. They were generous employers, kind and intelligent colleagues.

'Peter remembered all of them, all of us, in a poem he wrote just before he died. Here it is:

> Tonight I know that I will leave
> The fight is done
> And slowly as I say goodbye
> I need to speak
> And say my love for close-knit friends.
> Support, support was what they gave
> They made me live.
>
> To die, not old, cocooned in love
> Transferring through a point in time
> To somewhere else
> A gift we have no right to ask
> And it is mine.
>
> My brainwaves span the cool night air
> And tap goodbye to friends unseen.
> Will they go on and span in time
> My after life,
> I'd like to know.

'Peter was such a wonderful communicator with so much that was original to say; boy, did he think, and think again before coming up with structural solutions that made so much sense. I'd like to see Peter strolling up these stairs again today.'

Steelworker fettling gerberette in foundry, 1974.

# 6
# An engineer imagined
Kevin Barry

**P**eter Rice's *An Engineer Imagines* is not the first Irish memoir to place the birth of the protagonist relatively late in the narrative. Laurence Sterne, who was born in Clonmel, delayed the birth of his hero until Volume Three of *The Life and Opinions of Tristram Shandy*. Peter Rice, a native of Dundalk, was more restrained and delayed his hero's birth no later than Chapter Two. The dislocation is forceful: Chapter One is entitled 'Beaubourg' and recounts the design and construction of the Centre Pompidou in Paris, the decisive event that changed forever his professional life. Chapter Two throws events into reverse and leaves the heady 1970s for the earthier 1930s and 1940s to tell the story of his childhood and teenage years under the title 'Early Life'. This is just one of the surprises that give an unstable structure to *An Engineer Imagines*. Rice judged that his life began late, in France and not in Ireland, and the narrative's reversal of time provides a deliberate perspective in which his early life, remembered with a strong sense of anxiety and constraint, is placed at a distance. The suspense and delighted freedom of his success is, thereby, made all the more immediate. It would have been too painful to begin at the beginning.

Peter Rice, when diagnosed with an inoperable brain tumour, decided to write a memoir. His illness provided him with an urgent motive and spare time. Like many late acts of creation *An Engineer Imagines* is a work of collaboration. Peter Rice organized a team to help him achieve in book form the accumulated concept that defined who he was. Of all his partners and collaborators he was dying youngest: that would allow him the first word, but certainly not the last. He needed to ensure that younger engineers realized how he was special and what credit was due to him as an engineer who imagined. That they too might imagine. The title of the book, the moment it came to him with its simplicity and its rich double sense, pleased him enormously.

A young architect, Barbara Campbell, worked with him, taping conversations, preparing and editing transcriptions. Others helped provide images and select different kinds of paper. He was eager that the book be uneven, fragmentary, mixing chapters and cameos of unequal length and presentation. The change between the textures of the paper, rendering it tactile, made the book a material object. And though he did not succeed in getting the tracing paper he had wanted, to give an ephemeral presence to cameos such as the spider's web or the Frank Stella lattice, the project of a book provided a rare chance of fulfillment amidst uncertainty. Unlike the buildings that then preoccupied him, it could be completed in the limited time available. By contrast, the façade of the cathedral of Lille stood unfinished since 1854 and the window of translucent stone he had designed for it would not be in place until seven years after his death; Kansai International Airport still awaited its completion, built as it was on an artificial island requiring ten million man-hours for its construction; and the Full-Moon Theatre, where he would celebrate his last birthday on Bloomsday 1992, remained in his own words 'a project of many lifetimes'.

Peter Rice had been a child of County Louth in Ireland, a place he writes about without bitterness or affection. For many readers it appears that the words 'fear' and 'darkness' multiply across the page. The chapter has as epigraph a poem by local man Patrick Kavanagh, 'Inishkeen Road: July Evening'. Kavanagh, who had been an object of derision among his neighbours, became in the 1960s nationally celebrated as a poet. When Antoinette Quinn, a cousin of Peter Rice, published a study of Kavanagh's writing in 1991 Rice immediately ordered a copy. *An Engineer Imagines* records a moment when, as a child, he had noticed Kavanagh one summer's day: a man 'whom I would love to have to have known'; a man who 'could understand about being afraid. But then he was gone.'

The border between Northern Ireland and the Republic was only a few miles away and he remembered its anxious presence. As a child he would cycle with his brother Maurice on unapproved roads to cross the border and visit his mother's relatives who ran a shop in Crossmaglen. On both his mother's and his father's side Peter Rice was a child of the border counties. His maternal grandfather, Dada Quinn, was a schoolteacher in Inishkeen, Co. Monaghan. His paternal grandfather, born also in Co. Monaghan but stationed in Co. Kilkenny, was a member of the Royal Irish Constabulary, pensioned out of the force in his early forties. Peter Rice's mother, Maureen Quinn, was a brilliant student at University College Dublin. Her older brother William would rise through the ranks of the new national police force to become Commissioner of the Garda Síochána. Peter Rice's father, James, had been one of a handful of young men chosen during the period of transition to a new independent Irish state to study at the London School of Economics. He was deeply influenced by the socialist ethic and agnosticism he discovered there. The Rices did not subscribe to an Ireland of republican, Catholic, Gaelic nationalism. Traces of the Irish Civil War remained: James Rice and his wife Maureen came from families that had supported the 'pro-Treaty' Free State government, and had a tense relationship with their next door neighbours on Castle Road in Dundalk, a family suspected of participating during the Civil War in a 'republican' raid on the Quinn family home. James Rice used to urge his father-in-law Dada Quinn to read the *Observer*, and until the arrival of television the BBC Third Programme was always on during the evenings in the Rice household.

55

The landscape of his childhood, in Peter Rice's memory, had been a place in which 'Outside was more enclosed than inside ... You could go where you liked but you walked with fear, a permanent heavy shadow covered everything.' Although many who knew him as a boy speak about him as lively and athletic, a great swimmer who loved the outdoors, his own story of his childhood begins with a death, the death of his maternal grandfather, Dada Quinn, who had understood that mathematics are loveable. Death was commonplace and close. 'For a time I became an altar boy in Masses for the dead, every morning at eight o'clock in the small mortuary chapel, where the sweet smell of death and old women became almost addictive.' Even a visit to the home of his father's sisters, Nell and Moll, who lived with the older brother Uncle Frank in the leafy Dublin suburb of Mount Merrion, was touched with death. Frank Rice, serving with British forces in North Africa in World War I, brought back a memento: 'the unwrapped mummified hand and arm of a young Egyptian princess ... with gold-painted nails'. Beaubourg, after all this, could be counted as the first day of life alive.

Whenever Ireland is represented, or represents itself, as a backward and picturesque domain, it will appear unlikely that it should have produced a high-tech engineer such as Peter Rice, a furniture designer such as Eileen Gray, or a modernist architect such as Kevin Roche. The public mind has less difficulty with the notion of Irish writers, such as James Joyce or Samuel Beckett, bathing in the chill, invigorating waters of modernity. And this may be because the writers excavate an Irish past (the city of Dublin for Joyce, the Wicklow foothills for Beckett) and their writings revisit again and again the speech of the home place, its idioms and its cadences.

The work of an engineer, no less than that of a furniture designer or architect, has often appeared discontinuous with the public image and the self image of Irish culture. I know of no published list of key books by Irish authors of the twentieth century that includes *An Engineer Imagines*. After all, what link could there be between an Irish childhood and the ferro-cement leaves that filter light through the roof structure of the Menil

Gerberettes at the
Krupp foundry,
Saarbrücken
1974.

Collection museum in Houston, Texas; or the artisanal mirrors
that multiply a minima of light at Gourgoubès, on a south-facing
slope of the Massif Central, to illuminate the stage of Humbert
Camerlo's Full-Moon Theatre; or the choice of cast steel for the
gerberettes at Beaubourg?

In order to tell the story of the gerberette, with all the
suspense, momentary catastrophe and final success of this cast-
steel piece that defines Beaubourg, Peter Rice used the memoir
form of *An Engineer Imagines* to provide some kind of answer to
the question: why had he – the idiot of Beaubourg – against all
the odds been right to choose this material?

> One day shortly after the opening I saw an old lady,
> dressed in black like the Irish mothers of my youth,
> sitting perusing the people and looking in wide-
> eyed astonishment. I watched her for a while, just
> sitting quietly, stroking the side of the gerberette,
> she was not afraid, not intimidated and she was on
> the fourth floor.

The memoir form enabled Peter Rice to explain how his work was not what others, be they architects or bureaucrats, thought it to be. They imagined that, because he was an engineer, his motives were rational and sensible. Nothing, however, could have been less true. He chose cast steel because of a particular obsession (his word, not mine) about a sense of intimidation and fear that he found was all too common. Cast steel had a popular Victorian feel from its use in bridges, aqueducts, warehouses, and railway stations. And it carried the *traces de la main*, the trace or imprint of the workers who had made it. The path to be opened lay between two forms of intimidation: first, the intimidation that he remembered from his own dark childhood; and, second, that imposed in the wider world upon 'ordinary people' by temples of metropolitan style with their 'language of culture, alien and rigid and presumptive'. Beaubourg was designed to oppose these fears. Peter Rice was engaged in that futuristic space where technological innovation and social transformation join forces, a space most fully defined by Buckminster Fuller, the design engineer of the geodesic dome, whom Rice later celebrated when he adopted Fuller's term 'tensegrity' to describe the structure of the Pyramide Inversée at the Louvre.

So little did people arriving at Beaubourg feel fear or intimidation that, in its first decades, more visitors came to this building than to any other in Europe. The use of cast steel, the articulation and spacing of its discrete pieces, rendered the logic and the detail of the building warm, surprising, and clear. Success had depended upon an obsession to rid culture of fear within a complex process of collaboration between opposing styles: young people doing 'whatever we liked' and those 'analysis facilities available from highly skilled people with no emotional commitment to making the solutions work'.

If the economy of Beaubourg cancels fear, the ecology of the Full-Moon Theatre cancels darkness with the minima of light. 'La faiblesse', Rice replied to those who criticized the fragility of this project, 'c'est ici l'essentiel.' All those buildings that mediate transparency, those various systems for which Andy Sedgwick describes Rice as an engineer of light: the Grandes Serres at La Villette, Parc Citroën, the IBM Mobile Pavilion and lightweight semi-translucent structures such as Bari Stadium, and the inverted pyramid of the Louvre, these establish joyful exchanges between outside and inside. A cloud passing over the sun in the Houston sky, he noticed, will inflect however faintly the viewer's gaze within the Menil gallery. The high-tech present was to be used to rectify the past. Peter Rice's family often remark how, with the extraordinary gift-giving abundance of Christmas and the extravagance enjoyed on holidays with the children, he and Sylvia deliberately flung into reverse what they remembered as a frugal and austere childhood.

When Peter Rice asserts in *An Engineer Imagines* that nothing throughout his early life prepared him for the future he encountered, it is likely that his statement contributes to the notion that between Ireland and modernity there must always be something discontinuous, even incompatible. That would be to misunderstand the nature of Rice's memoir, which is entirely local in its reference: local to the hinterland of his childhood. Were Rice to be addressing a larger scene, that is Ireland between 1935, the year of his birth, and 1955, the year he emigrated, there would be need to describe a country that was also a centre for exciting individual and state-sponsored architectural and engineering innovation. International modernism in its various styles informed much public debate and was found at many new popular venues: the Collinstown Airport Terminal (1940), the Hospital Sweepstakes Offices (1937), the Michael Scott house (1938), the Irish Pavilion at the New York World Fair (1939), and the intense public and professional controversy and celebration of the Central Bus Station Busáras (1944–53). Indeed it was Busáras that brought Ove Arup to Ireland where in 1946, the same year as in London, he first established an office under the title Ove N. Arup Consulting Engineers. Peter Rice, the son of a modernizing public servant, could not have remained ignorant of this new vitality and the extraordinarily aware young teams of designers that gathered around impresario architects such as Desmond FitzGerald and Michael Scott. At boarding school in Newbridge College, Co. Kildare, Rice was also exposed to the strong contemporary work of the sculptor Henry Flanagan OP, a member of the teaching staff who in the midst of the schoolboys carved in the schoolyard. Another distinguished graduate of Newbridge College, Philip

59

O'Kane, Professor of Engineering at University College Cork, has observed that as a teenager Peter Rice would have had early direct experience of the primary value of the *traces de la main* in watching Henry Flanagan working in timber and stone.

In the final pages of *An Engineer Imagines* Peter Rice describes, in anticipation of his early death, how Gourgoubès, the site of the Full-Moon Theatre, 'will eventually become my spiritual home, that part of me which is not in Ireland'. The memoir shifts between these two locales that haunted him, one the inverse of the other, but both irreducibly recalcitrant places. At Gourgoubès, through artisanal teamwork, something was built that delighted him because it contradicted so many contemporary assumptions. The Full-Moon Theatre proposed that more can be done with less; that it may be better to think small; that there is no hurry to succeed; that a single work may take many lifetimes; that design ought to be fun; that the local and unforeseen win out when 'the bloody wind came from the other direction' to blow the lightweight mirrors away. Finally, the Full-Moon Theatre proposed the pleasures of failure: that something, even when designed by the best engineers, is imperfect, that it does not immediately work, that 'it's awkward and it will always be awkward, which actually in the end I like'.

In the archives at Gourgoubès is the typescript of an unfinished play, 'The Bridge', which Peter Rice wrote towards the end of his life. In these pages an engineer imagines returning to his home place to set things right, to find a solution, to rectify the past and reverse history, to build a bridge between the two warring communities, Catholics and Protestants: 'a clean white bridge gleaming in the sun … a symbol of a future without fear'. Once home the engineer discovers that he is not wanted, that his community does not wish for this kind of change, that his enlightenment adventure only makes matters worse, and that his return, so passionately desired by himself, is rejected even by those he loves most intensely. The fantasy is Gothic, dead-end and almost guilt-ridden. 'The Bridge' renders a private and haunting fear that 'home' too had been his place but that he had no place there. In a poem of the 1970s, 'Afterlives', the Belfast poet Derek Mahon wondered:

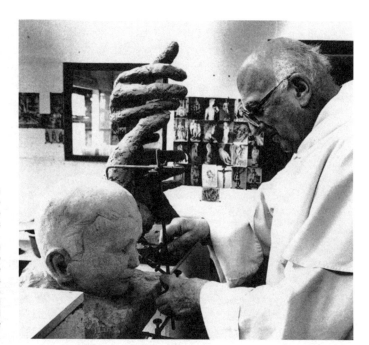

Henry Flanagan working in his studio at Newbridge College where Peter Rice was a pupil from 1951–3. The 'Head of a Young Boy' dates from the early 1950s; the Renaissance images on the wall were on display to pupils and the mirror served to backlight sculpted pieces.

Perhaps if I'd stayed behind
And lived it bomb by bomb
I might have grown up at last
And learnt what is meant by home.

It is an emotion hazarded by many of the generation who emigrated from Ulster and the border counties during a period of inter-community violence that ran in parallel to the years of Peter Rice's professional success.

*An Engineer Imagines* contains the history and the immense joy of that success. The memoir deliberately aimed to establish his credo and his credit among future generations of engineers, a project that was achievable and achieved during the last months of his life. Above all, the memoir celebrates the one element, never surely knowable, as the means to achieve a rupture between the past and a better future: the element, scarcely imaginable, of surprise.

A pivotal moment for Ed Clark, with his father and younger brother at Lloyd's, London c.1986.

Selfridges (Future Systems), Birmingham 2003.

# Ed Clark

SADLY I NEVER actually met Peter. I joined Arup too late. My decision to become a structural engineer had been largely inspired by a family trip to the Lloyd's building shortly after it opened in 1986. I was a teenager at the time and only later discovered that it had been engineered by Arup and then learnt about Peter and his role in its creation. I read *An Engineer Imagines* as a student and still have above my desk today a passage found at the back of the book about surprise and keeping the nose to the ground.

When I joined Arup as a graduate my 'apprentice' relationship with David Glover was similar to the relationship he'd had with Peter, so I feel like I inherited some of his guidance second hand. It's difficult to describe what I mean by that, but I guess it manifests itself as an attitude to work: making the most of every project; that balance of creativity, pragmatism and rigour; an inquisitiveness and courage to experiment, to go beyond the standard solution if that's what's required to get the best, most resolved, highest-value solution.

The best example of this from my own career to date has to be the sprayed concrete façade of Selfridges, Birmingham. David and I were trying to live up to Peter's legacy in the eyes of Jan Kaplicky at Future Systems. To spray the façade was David's idea; it was the right one and I had to make it work. It's not exactly the ferro-cement leaves at the Menil Collection museum but was arrived at by keeping our noses to the ground in the way Peter recommended.

Still image of Ian Ritchie, Peter Rice and Martin Francis (RFR), from *La Cité en Lumière*,1986.

7

# The Peter Rice I knew

Ian Ritchie

From the start of our professional relationship in 1978, when Peter invited me to work with him in Arup's Lightweight Structures Group, which he led, we got on very well, and soon became friends as well as colleagues. Living close to him in west London, I often joined his family to support Queen's Park Rangers FC at home matches. Our professional relationship and private friendship flourished because we trusted each other. We knew that if either of us was in trouble the other would not walk away – quite the opposite. We would hang together to sort things out. At RFR, the design-engineering partnership we formed in 1981 with Martin Francis, it was the same. That loyalty and straightforwardness gave RFR immense underlying strength to take on challenges and not be deflected in the pursuit of excellence.

From my conversations with Peter, it was clear he felt hugely indebted to Ove Arup, and also to Jack Zunz. Both saw in Peter someone special, someone to be nurtured. It was the strength-in-depth of Ove Arup and Partners that provided Peter with a professional base and support, and gave him the space and time to develop, explore and manifest his extraordinary abilities. He learned from Ove Arup, who spoke and wrote a lot about collaboration, that teamwork is crucial. But at the same time, for Peter, there was no doubt that individual professional responsibility was an important factor to be recognized by each participant in a project. Although no one person owns the solution in any truly collaborative venture, Peter believed – and lived out his belief – that, at crucial stages in a project, individuals must assume responsibility according to their knowledge, skill and wisdom.

I can illustrate this with a vivid memory of a conversation over dinner with Martin and Peter at the Brasserie de la Gare du Nord, not long after we had formed RFR. I told the story of my sense of defeat, when working with Norman Foster on the Sainsbury Centre, at not finding a way of supporting the glass end walls of the building using vertical cable bracing. At the time we were working on a solution for bracing the glass of the La Villette 'bioclimatic façades'. To overcome the optical solidity in daylight of glass fins, when viewed at an angle, I suggested that an ideal answer was to replace the glass fins with a horizontal cable arrangement. I sketched a diagram, explaining that, as we looked from side to side, it would be good to keep the horizontal view empty. The cables, spaced two metres apart, would lightly frame different panoramas depending on the level the viewer was at inside the museum, and with reduced visual interference we would get closer to the idea of transparency. 'Stop!' Peter said. 'Don't say any more. I'll find the answer. Give me a couple of weeks.' It took nearly two years of design and intense analysis, at no small cost, to produce the final answer, but the façades were built as imagined.

Although he influenced many architectural projects, Peter would never accept he acted beyond his own professional remit. He felt that professional prejudice and the boundaries it created were unacceptable obstacles to sharing in the creative and inventive process of the built environment. But he had techniques for collaboration that preserved the distinctions be-tween engineering and architecture on some projects. Although he worked with many architects, often he remained distant from direct dialogue, and would place another engineer between him and architects who were perhaps less open and relaxed than he was in the shared formulation of concepts. And he would do the same thing on occasions when the project was not interesting enough to deflect him from those with whom he was more deeply engaged. I watched him master the art of politely bringing a conversation to a close, either to make way for his next meeting or to secure moments for personal reflection and quiet. Peter could have a mischievous manner, a well-camouflaged hint of inner enjoyment at being sought out by worldly-wise architects arriving at his door. He did not like bullshit, shallowness or arrogance and had little interest in self-centred professionals interested only in the superficialities.

Peter felt that in the right kind of collaboration the architect brought creativity, together with an attitude, opinions and preferences, while the engineer introduced an element of technical exploration and hence invention. These observations indicated a concern for the engineer's identity in a post-war environment dominated by architecture, and disguised a far more important factor: the need for spirituality, given the lack of it in our present age. There is no doubt that as Peter gained the respect of architects and grew in confidence he felt all the more that he was engineer, licensed dreamer and poet.

We often talked about the need for contemporary architecture to embody sensual expressions that the ordinary person could feel, communicating more than just a *coup visuel.* Peter had his own phrase for this: les traces de la main. This, in essence, was the 'bespoke' contribution that an architect – or engineer – could give to any piece of the architecture – and hence to the whole building: the need for content and meaning within the visible and material construction. This is one of Rice's lasting legacies to architecture – certainly to me. An engineer is not simply one who computes and engineers a solution. In his search for quality he has a moral obligation to bring a deeper understanding, insight and contribution to the built environment. For this reason, an engineer also has to be aware of political context. Peter knew this and, using charm, reason and silence, was skilled at helping to bring ideas (not only his own) to fruition with clients.

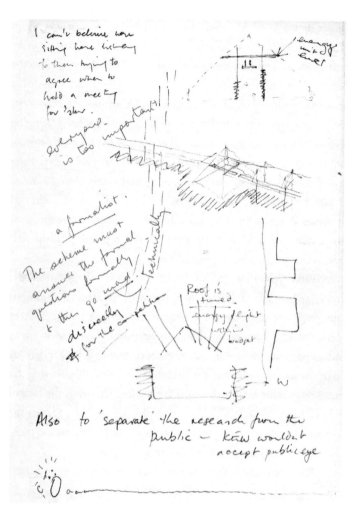

Two pages from
Ian Ritchie's 'Black
Book 5' on which
he and Peter Rice
silently 'discuss'
a Kew Gardens
Competition,
during a meeting
in Paris on 20
February 1983.

He was genuinely interested in society, in particular the world of construction and the importance of the built environment to society, as part of our cultural legacy. On this we were in tune and did not need lengthy conversations to explain why one particular strategy or idea should be adopted rather than another. We would talk longer about other things: life, our families, football, writers and society. We never discussed projects he was doing with other architects. I hugely respected this integrity and discretion, a hallmark of his character.

We discussed those moments in a professional career when things go seriously wrong, and how people's behaviour can reveal

69

their true character. He once related the events of a horrendous weekend in Paris, immediately after the Krupps factory sent word that the first gerberette for the Centre Pompidou had developed internal cracks (he told me this in confidence, and he would not have wished me to divulge his thoughts and memories of that weekend). At this moment of crisis he received a call telling him that his mother was gravely ill. He flew to Ireland.

Peter always gave space to others: he had an open door and an open mind, which is why there was always a queue outside his office of both young and established architects from around the world. His generosity with his time became legendary; even his immediate colleagues at Ove Arup and Partners and at RFR in Paris had to join the queue now and again. During the RFR years it was my good fortune to enjoy his company, together with a meal and decent bottle of wine, on flights between London and Paris; this meant that I didn't have to queue up to talk to him! Peter made time for the events of the day itself, despite the fact that he had obligations to fulfil. He was always faithful to his commitments. How he managed to find time and space for his work, colleagues and private life is something of a mystery, for he was not the most organized individual. His secretaries at Arup, Sheila and later Caroline, would sometimes ring up to ask me if the pile of paper on his desk was a real project, and whether it was one of Peter's or one of mine! Peter chose to spend little time on management.

There were moments when he simply folded up, tired. In 1987 Peter and I were invited to attend a meeting in Paris to discuss a design concept for the World Fair in Seville, scheduled for 1992. The request came from Pippo Lionni, a designer, writer and teacher, who had a background in mathematics and philosophy. He was already involved with Dièse, a firm of social anthropologist consultants, who had been shortlisted to prepare a tangible idea for the Spanish Pavilion of the Future. They had little idea of the implications of realizing something physical, but they could certainly talk the talk. At one point in the meeting there was a thud – Peter's head had hit the table and he was fast asleep! Moments like these are unforgettable.

I loved Peter first and foremost because of his personality. He was open-minded, generous, and never allowed his pro-fessional prowess and formidable skills in engineering and mathematics to become barriers to knowing him. And he never blew his own trumpet. He possessed an ego but, despite his ever-growing reputation, he never let it disorientate him or overwhelm others, and he was an exemplary mentor. All he asked in return was that people should be themselves; he couldn't tolerate pretence, artificiality or conceit. What was so attractive was his simplicity and openness, which were not only disarming but enlightening. These characteristics were patent in the sheer joy he conveyed on receiving the RIBA Gold Medal, when two of his most treasured friends openly expressed their indebtedness to him, while his immediate and extended family bathed in the warmth of the occasion.

Around Peter was his family and their presence underpinned Peter's confidence and values as a person. They allowed him to be the very special engineer he was, one of those rare people who became a professional friend to many. That's why he is missed so much – for his engineering intellect, but perhaps more because he was such a wonderful individual. He will remain an inspiration to many working in architecture and engineering, art, drama and music, fields in which he walked with humility and the curiosity of a child.

71

The Broken Jug, Frank Stella, 2001.

# 8
# Working with Peter Rice and Frank Stella
Martin Francis

I first met Peter Rice in the offices of Piano & Rogers in Paris at the time when the detailing started on Beaubourg. Because I had been working on glass walls with Norman Foster, I was asked by Richard Rogers to consult on the façades of some of the adjacent buildings around the piazza. At Foster's Willis Faber building at Ipswich we had achieved a 4000m² suspended toughened-glass curtain around the free-form shape of the building. Years later, when Adrien Fainsilber won the competition for the National Museum of Science and Technology at La Villette he invited Peter Rice to collaborate on the special structures of the project. Fainsilber wanted to do glass like Foster. So Peter brought me on board and I suggested we include Ian Ritchie, a close friend whom I had got to know at Foster's. Together we formed RFR.

Fainsilber's project contained three *façades bioclimatiques*, each 32 metres by 32 metres, which formed buffer spaces between the park and the Museum. Transparency was the primary design requirement. There were no intermediate floors to provide bracing and we looked at several options for supporting the glass, including the glass fins used at Ipswich. However, over lunch one day, I mentioned to Peter that toughened glass is a flexible material, and showed him an advertisement that displayed two trestles supporting a 3mm sheet of toughened glass. A child on a tricycle sat in the middle of the glass sheet, which had a deflection of about 15cm. Immediately Peter had a 'eurêka' moment exclaiming 'If that is the case then we don't need a rigid supporting frame and if we don't need a rigid frame, then we can use a cable-truss system.' Thus the now commonly used cable-braced glass wall was born. To this day people look at the horizontal cable system at La Villette and think that it cannot be stable and that it must flip over. This is just one of many examples of Peter's ability to see beyond the apparently logical solution to a problem.

After the façades at La Villette were completed, being preoccupied with a large yacht project, I became a sleeping partner at RFR, and Ian left to set up his architectural practice in London. Peter continued with RFR and worked on the canopies in the Parc de La Villette with Bernard Tschumi and a range of other projects in Paris. Our friendship continued. Years later, although at the height of his powers and jetting round Europe to work with Richard in London, Renzo in Genoa, Paul Andreu in Paris, Peter dropped everything to help me when I asked him about unforeseen vibration problems on an ECO (a cutting-edge high-speed motor yacht we were testing). Only a month later he telephoned me to tell me that he had been diagnosed with a brain tumour and could no longer travel He asked me if I could resume the direction of RFR.

While I was again working at RFR I received a call from Henry Bardsley, one of RFR's longest serving engineers, to ask me to help on a project with Frank Stella. I was aware of Frank's relationship with Peter Rice and with the Groningen project, but I had not worked on it nor met Frank before. This new project was a sculpture for the Ritz Carlton Millennium Hotel in Singapore.

The scale of the project was quite small and I suggested that it be built empirically, without advanced calculation, by artisan boat-builders whom I knew in Antibes. They could work with

Sculpture,
Ritz Carlton
Millennium Hotel
Singapore,
Frank Stella,
1998.

wood, stainless steel and fibreglass in complex shapes. This was
the first project deriving from Peter Rice's work with Frank Stella
that was actually built. Up to then all collaborations, including
that for the Groningen Museum, had remained at project stage.

The original project that brought Peter and Frank together
was an idea for a footbridge across the Seine in Paris. In his
introductory note to *An Engineer Imagines* Frank Stella recalled
how he had built a model, three metres wide, that when enlarged
was meant to span the Seine. To Peter Rice he addressed the
question, 'Do you think it's buildable?'

He looked at the model of the bridge again and responded 'Yes.' I didn't believe him for a second. Then I began to realize what that 'Yes' meant. Sure it was buildable – buildable by him, not me. But, fortunately, there was more to it than that. Somehow, even though he communicated a questioning, perhaps conditional sense of approval, he did it in such a way that the recollection makes me happy to this moment. It seems the 'Yes' implied that the model might be worth developing if we could work it through; if, first, I could only make myself clear about my idea for the bridge.

In the end this project did not get very far but it became the catalyst for an all too short but fruitful collaboration between the two, the legacy of which continues today in the work that I have been privileged to do with Frank. The project for the Groningen Museum was the most developed of many ideas Peter and Frank worked on. It remained close to Stella's heart, and he vividly related how he had arrived at the concept:

A simple, communicable idea popped out at me from a Dover book of Chinese lattice designs. Twisting one of its leaf shapes made a wonderful roof plane for our building model. When Peter asked me what was the idea behind the wavy roof I could say proudly, 'It's like a leaf.' Once he had a handle, once he could grasp the image, Peter just rolled on like a juggernaut, crushing the obstacles of practicality and cost, making it possible for us to build what we liked.

Before we had the opportunity to approach the Groningen project again, I worked with RFR and Frank Stella on a number of other projects of ever-increasing size and complexity. 'The Broken Jug' was the first large-scale fully engineered structure that we built; it was designed to resist hurricane force winds and salt spray on a coastal site. It is 15 metres wide by 11 metres high,

Model for Project
Across the Seine
River, Paris, Frank
Stella, 1988.

weighs 45 tons, and is built in aluminum. For the first time we demonstrated that we could engineer and build a complex non-linear form using the skill set of the shipbuilding industry.

Now we were in a position to approach the Groningen project using our acquired knowledge and computing skills. Some small steel prototype sections were made and, after some years, Frank Stella decided to revisit the project with a larger version that we called the 'Groningen Leaves'. We had no computer files of the original project, only the largely hand-made 'black model' which itself is a precursor of other maquettes.

Since the development of the original idea between Frank and Peter, CAD software had developed considerably, so working with a developer I was able to create a parametric model of the project. This enabled Frank to change the shaping and get results in real time. We were able then to use rapid prototyping to produce models in a few days.

Seduced by the possibilities of these new tools, Frank developed a large number of ever more complex small sculptures, but wanted to build 'the leaves' as a full-sized building that one could walk through, or under, or even live in. The engineering challenges returned with the increase in scale and more than ever I missed Peter's ability to simplify the problems or to translate the questions. Frank had decided that he would like to build 'the leaves' in carbon fibre and acquired a five-axis numerically controlled milling machine to make the foam cores that would subsequently be wrapped in fibreglass and carbon. We worked with Arup to determine the required material thickness and jointing system. Because it was 'a work of art' we would have to be able to get it

77

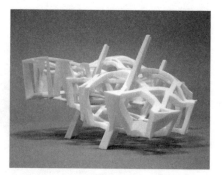

into a gallery, assemble it, stop it collapsing on the public and then remove it, hopefully to the site of a collector.

Frank was invited to exhibit simultaneously during 2007 two shows at The Metropolitan Museum of Art in New York: one was 'Frank Stella on the Roof' and the other, a retrospective, 'Frank Stella: Painting into Architecture'. We therefore commissioned a boat-builder, 'an expert in carbon fibre' based in Brazil, to make a two-thirds scale version for the roof exhibition, and this acquired the title 'The Chinese Pavilion'.

The two versions were delivered to the Metropolitan Museum. 'The Chinese Pavilion' was hoisted onto the roof in an unfinished state.

The full-sized version, also partly completed, was installed in the gallery. In this instance we placed it emerging from the wall of the exhibition space, to allow for the movement of people around it. This piece was called 'The Ship'.

Both pieces are true to the spirit of the original Groningen project and demonstrate the challenge construction of such pieces present.

When I am asked what imprint Peter Rice has left on Frank Stella's work I reply with two thoughts. Peter gave Frank the confidence to create ever more complex works with no constraints of form or scale; he always said, 'Yes it is possible.' As part of Frank's team trying to build these pieces I am sure that, had Peter still been with us, a Chinese Pavilion would stand in Hyde Park and a Broken Jug in Central Park, and probably a great deal more.

We miss you Peter.

**LEFT**
Model of Groningen Museum Project, Frank Stella, 1989.

**RIGHT**
Model of The Ship, Frank Stella, 2004.

The Chinese Pavilion, Frank Stella, 2007.

The Ship, Frank Stella, 2007.

**ABOVE**
Flow, glass,
plaster and
bronze, Vivienne
Roche, Fingal
Council Chamber,
Dublin 2002.

**LEFT**
NC Iris, stainless
steel and lighting,
Vivienne Roche,
Mayor Square,
Dublin 2006.

# Vivienne Roche

DURING MY CAREER I have thought of Peter Rice's memoir, *An Engineer Imagines*, as my bible. Many of my large-scale projects start with a re-reading of this book, which helps to reinforce a sense of ambition before embarking on something new. The interplay of text and image demonstrates the search for the authentic character of a material, which Peter Rice says is at the heart of engineering design.

Combining and using materials in new ways is part of what I do, and a continuing engagement with engineering principles seems natural to me. This may be obvious in steel sculptures such as *NC Iris* (Mayor Square, Dublin), where I worked in a creative collaboration with Arup, but it is equally true of the slumped glass and stucco plaster of *Flow* (Fingal County Hall, Dublin). The geometry of moving water can be expressed in glass or bronze, with time becoming an underlying part of such a work's structure.

Through a series of large-scale drawings of crafted and structural details of Peter Rice's work in Paris, I am engaged in a process to reveal more about the variety of materials that hold our attention in his buildings. The drawings are grouped under the title 'The Eye is Final', a reference to how the eye perceives tactile and other sensual qualities of outstanding engineering. Though Rice himself under-rated his own ability to draw, he knew that drawing has subtle powers of 'showing' that elude photography.

Fingal County Hall entrance atrium (Bucholz McEvoy/RFR), Swords, Co. Dublin, 2000.

# 9

# Commodious vicus of recirculation

Seán Ó Laoire

our words from the beginning of *Finnegans Wake* as a title for an essay on Peter Rice may seem to reinforce a stereotype of achievement by people born in Ireland as centered inevitably on great literature. My emphasis, however, is on how these words convey the Vitruvian ideal of 'building well', the notion of a journey, and of cyclical reconnection: themes that are interwoven in this essay. To speak of traces, in English or in French, is to convey a sense of a mark (*trace de la main*), a remnant, a path, a vestige, and of the layers between and beneath each of the words: 'commodius vicus of recirculation'.

If birthplace, environment and cultural formation shape us, I am prompted, as a fellow Irishman to place his genius and genesis in context. The monotonic, isolated Ireland that he left, with so many thousand others, is changed utterly. In the landscape of his childhood, once the setting for an episode of an ancient Irish myth-cycle, there is evidence that tribal enmities are softening. Part of that cathartic process has been the belated acknowledgment of how many Irish families, tribally Catholic and nominally nationalist, had given service to the British empire, both in Ireland and abroad. In the wake of the 'Celtic Tiger', Ireland is struggling to redefine itself. Part of that redefinition centers on false oppositions between Arts and Sciences, and invites an interrogation of a self-image of Irishness still defined by the notion of a dominant gene that facilitates a production-line of poets, writers, singers and storytellers.

Like most of my peers at the School of Architecture at University College Dublin in the turbulent late 1960s, I was tribally Catholic, culturally nationalist and the beneficiary of parents of the first generation of 'nation builders' who shared a commitment to their children's education. For me the journey of interrogation had started in the mid 1970s and was given renewed urgency by my only meeting with Peter Rice, after a lecture he gave in the city of Limerick, part of a voluntary speaking tour of Ireland he generously undertook a few years before his death. In Ireland at large this interrogation has yet to embrace Peter Rice as the role model he ought to become.

Ireland had been from the eighteenth century a peripheral agrarian island linked by complex ties to that powerhouse of the industrial revolution across the water. Irish no less than Scottish engineers were among the great pioneers of that 'British' epoch, and such was its reach that even France deferred. Glasgow manufacturers created the cast-iron structure of the Gare du Nord in Paris.

The remit and range of the great nineteenth-century engineers straddled architecture, engineering and construction in works as diverse as harbours, canals, aqueducts, railways and large-span, cast-iron structures. Peter Rice cited the great achievements of those engineers as an inspiration to his own development. The Ireland where Rice grew up still bears the imprint of Scottish-born engineers such as John Rennie (1761–1821) and Alexander Nimmo (1783–1832), and of many Irish-born engineers such as Bindon Blood Stoney (1828–1909) and Robert Mallett (1810–81), whose formation was linked to the industrial revolution. Dundalk hosted a substantial iron foundry and railway works, and was also the birthplace of one of the great railway engineers of nineteenth-century Ireland, Sir John Benjamin McNeill

(1793–1880). Ireland's foremost railway engineer of that period, William Dargan (1799–1867), was of Catholic stock and the product of a local Co. Carlow 'hedge school', where his talents were recognized and supported by benign Protestant merchants. Both McNeill and Dargan worked for Thomas Telford (1757–1834), the Scottish engineer and sometime poet, known in his lifetime as 'The Colossus of Roads'.

When Peter Rice arrived to study engineering in Belfast in the 1950s the city still throbbed to an industrial heartbeat, cities of the Irish Republic still fatalistically exporting cattle and a largely unskilled population. The accession of Ireland to EEC membership in 1973 inspired some of my generation to work in continental Europe. Only in retrospect can I see that my work as a young architect in Milan allowed me some years later to understand and appreciate my compatriot Peter Rice, and to understand how serendipity shapes the making and journey of ideas, and how the formation of an individual can determine their capacity to answer the beckonings of fate: in Peter Rice's case to enter a nexus of traditions, histories, and cultures, tempering innovation and technology with enduring humanity.

My employer in Milan was Vittorio Gregotti, then a prolific contributor to the architectural design magazine *Casabella*, as famously was Ernesto Nathan Rogers, an architect of Milan's shrine to modern Italian Rationalism, the Torre Valesca, and a cousin of the emerging 'British' architect Richard Rogers. Ernesto Rogers was also a teacher in the Politecnico di Milano from which, in 1964, Lorenzo 'Renzo' Piano graduated as an architect. A trans-generational, trans-cultural and trans-national convergence built Beaubourg: Richard Rogers, Lorenzo 'Renzo' Piano, Gianfranco Francini, Peter Rice, and Ove Arup, an English-born Danish-Norwegian. This was a defining event and the Centre Pompidou served as a catalyst in a heated discourse on architectural theory. It can be read as a hybridized descendant of new building typologies that emerged in nineteenth-century Europe: popular mass exhibition buildings, museums and public libraries. Its radical expression, however, and its ambition, which was both republican and egalitarian, connect it to the lineage of the populist, cutting-edge structures of the nineteenth century, however 'imperialist' they may have been: London's Crystal Palace (1851), and the Grand Palais of Paris (1897–1900). Peter Rice's remark in praise of the Grand Palais – 'that it is so fine and that we have failed to do as well since' – demonstrates his attachment to that epoch.

The first precursor of the modern World Fair was held in Paris on the Champ de Mars in 1798. This was also the year that Richard Turner was born to an Anglo-Irish Iron founder family in Dublin, a city then at the apex of its neo-classical pomp, and the second city of the British empire. If the island of Rice's birth produced his spiritual ancestor it is Richard Turner. At his foundry at Ballsbridge in Dublin Turner developed prefabricated curvilinear glass, and cast- and wrought-iron structures of exceptional elegance, such as the Palm House at Kew Gardens, London, and the Curvilinear Range at the Botanic Gardens, Dublin. Turner was the designer and constructor of another emerging typology that would equally fascinate Peter Rice: the railway 'shed', including those at Broadstone, Dublin, and Lime Street, Liverpool. Turner, nothing if not a visionary, produced proposals for a Channel Tunnel. He was an under-bidder for Joseph Paxton's Crystal Palace.

The Crystal Palace formed a central part of the Great Exhibition of 1851 that was a riposte to France's tenth World Fair, or French Industrial Exposition, of 1844. Symbolically it represented the apex of Victoria's empire, and also it delineated the lines for the combatants in the so-called 'Battle of the Styles' – which dominated architectural and engineering discourse until well into the twentieth century. Arguing the merits of 'Classicism' versus 'Gothic', and their fitness to specific building types, both sides were at one in their virulent rejection of any 'hi-tech' future prompted by the Crystal Palace and its attendant associations with the Industrial Revolution.

Fast forward then to the Centre Pompidou in the 1970s, a building whose roots are deep in British and European avant-garde movements, notably the 'Archigram' radicals of the 1960s based at the Architectural Association. Like the Crystal Palace, the Centre Pompidou also delineated battle lines, articulated by theorists such as Robert Venturi and Charles Jencks.

Stack A, detail of river-facing façade counterpointing John Rennie's cast-iron structure (Michael Collins Associates/RFR), IFSC Docklands, Dublin 2007.

In the Centre Pompidou, and in his life's output, Peter Rice instinctively embraced the principles of the early Roman architect and engineer, Vitruvius. If Firmness, Commodity and Delight are the essential elements of Vitruvian 'well building', his contribution as an engineer was to ensure that Firmness and Commodity were the servants of Delight – the synthesis of great architecture. In his work with Arup, with the Renzo Piano Building Workshop, and with RFR, he consistently focused his genius on turning problems into poems, collaboratively in the service of a shared vision – be that in his singular contribution to the development of planar glazing or in the orchestration of materiality with elegant graceful structure. The traces of Peter Rice's work are now widespread and happily evident also in Ireland.

In Dublin's docklands, Michael Collins Associates collaborated with RFR in the restoration of 'Stack A' at the Custom House Quay. It was constructed circa 1820 to a design by John Rennie, a prolific and versatile Scottish engineer who had earlier collaborated with David Asher Alexander on the design in 1811 of the still-remarkable 'Tobacco Dock' in London's docklands. 'Stack A' today counterpoints the signature, elegant 'structural glazing' developed by Rice with Rennie's radically innovative cast-iron roof structure, symmetrically linking great engineers through time and place.

RFR collaborated with architects Bucholz McEvoy, in the design of County Halls in Limerick, Mullingar and Fingal, and in the design of elegant 'Welcoming Pavilions' at the entrace to Leinster House, which houses Dáil Eireann, the Irish Houses of Parliament. There is a fitting and poetic eloquence in these acts of reconnection and collaboration – with Rice's legacy gracing the public realm of civic space in Ireland. In all cases the architectural aspiration is to embody ideals of public engagement and transparency in government. The 'Welcoming Pavilions', while clearly having a familial connection to the conservatories in Parc Citroën, defer to the neo-classical curtilage of Leinster House.

The striking and well-tempered façades of the county halls in Limerick, Mullingar and Fingal all mediate their settings with generous and elegant atria, while their detailing and materiality is recognizably an evolution of Rice's vocabulary, refined in

89

Stack A interior (Michael Collins Associates/RFR), IFSC Docklands, Dublin 2007.

Welcoming Pavilion (Bucholz McEvoy/RFR), Dáil Eireann, Leinster House, Dublin 2006.

collaboration with talented architects. In the Council Chamber in Fingal County Hall is a majestic mural in plaster, glass and bronze by Vivienne Roche, one of Ireland's leading artists and sculptors. The daughter of an engineer and long-time collaborator with Arup, her work is a direct response to the values implicit in Peter Rice's legacy.

When I visited Humbert Camerlo and his Full-Moon Theatre at Gourgoubès in the mid 1990s, it was in the process of benign decay, and that in a vivid way magnified its intention to be a womb for artistic rebirth, as grasses invaded the dry-stone amphitheatre steps, and the slightly battered silhouettes of 'lunar' reflectors stood against the big night sky of the Massif Central. Gourgoubès is a primal place. I indulged momentarily in the possibility that it was these fragments of a magic project that linked this place and Ireland in Rice's heart.

I was also reminded of a childhood 'role model' of the young Rice at Inishkeen, the poet Patrick Kavanagh, who wrote in the poem 'Epic' about the Second World War and the isolation of a 'neutral' Ireland from Europe:

> I inclined
> To lose my faith in Ballyrush and Gortin
> Till Homer's ghost came whispering to my mind.
> He said: 'I made the Iliad from such
> A local row. Gods make their own importance.'

Peter Rice's legacy transcends its origins. Nowhere is this more eloquently embodied than in Gourgoubès, a project and a place that is ephemeral, poetic, beyond ego: at once primal, innovative, creative and cosmic – subordinate both to nature and the trace of his hand.

Peter Rice, *An Engineer Imagines*, 1994.

# Barbara Campbell-Lange

THE MAKING OF Peter's book *An Engineer Imagines* was a project made possible by the generosity of many invisible hands and minds.

It was a surprise when Peter asked me to work with him and we invented a way of working as we went along. My involvement was to work with him on the core ideas and structure of the book: it very deliberately avoids a conventional linear narrative of his life and projects, focusing instead on the essential conceptual issues associated with each project in a way that could be taken forward by others. It intersperses the 'cameos' (one-page idea projects) amongst the longer chapters at unexpected points (as far as book production would allow) and discusses the nature of physical and metaphysical relationships throughout. It was my greatest pleasure and honour to have worked with him. I recall it vividly. Indeed those months I spent working with Peter, the conversations about each project, have profoundly influenced my work as an architect and teacher. The final paragraph in the book, where Peter talks about surprise, I taped when we were sitting together on the sofa in the Rice's living room, with the family dog, the piece Frank Stella had given him as a gift propped up nearby and laps full of transcripts and handwritten notes: he understood the importance of following and committing to the essential elements of any situation or project, no matter where it might lead, for the result would always reveal something unexpected, something new, something true.

Centre Pompidou-Metz (Shigeru Ban, Jean de Gastines, Philip Gumuchdjian), Metz 2010.

## 10
# Listening to the idea
Sophie Le Bourva

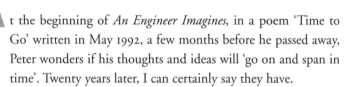t the beginning of *An Engineer Imagines*, in a poem 'Time to Go' written in May 1992, a few months before he passed away, Peter wonders if his thoughts and ideas will 'go on and span in time'. Twenty years later, I can certainly say they have.

I met Peter in 1988 in his Paris office. I was an engineering and architecture student at the time. I had an engineering degree from the Ecole Polytechnique in Paris. After Polytechnique, because it is a very generalist scientific college, students tend to specialize. I had by then developed an interest in civil engineering and my long love of anything related to the visual arts led me to architecture. I decided to do two degrees in parallel, architecture and civil engineering; one at the Ecole des Ponts et Chaussées and the other at the Ecole d'Architecture, Paris La Seine. Combined degrees did not exist and to study two disciplines was rare.

Having trained as an engineer and an architect, I was looking for a space to operate in both, perhaps in order to postpone making a choice between them. There were not many places where this could be envisaged or that would value the double qualification. Most firms wanted you to be either an engineer or an architect. Peter, on the other hand, was interested by the interaction of the two disciplines. In his Paris office both architects and engineers worked side by side to deliver projects. I was later to discover that Peter's Arup group also included different disciplines, as structural and services engineers worked together on projects. That was a different balance of disciplines, but the idea of integrating a variety of disciplines was present in both workplaces. Initially I was attracted by Peter's concept of such a working environment. I felt at the time that I would not have to choose between the two disciplines although I realized later that joining Peter's team was in fact to make the choice to be a structural engineer.

It was after a long chase that I managed to meet Peter, as he was very much in demand and his administrator was very protective of his time. When we met we got on well and he offered me a job first in his Paris office and later at Arup. He liked enthusiastic, flexible, strong, young people. Peter's structural team was formed of young people, generally between twenty-five and thirty-five years old. Many years after his death, I coined the phrase 'the Peter babies' to describe these young people. He was deliberately using our youth, our energy and our lack of prejudices to make rather unusual things happen. He never articulated this and it seemed quite normal at the time. It probably reflected his own experience on the Sydney Opera House, where he was given lots of responsibilities early on. Of course later on, when he felt you needed to leave the nest, when you had developed a fuller knowledge of engineering, he would push you into the world.

Challenges would be thrown at you and you had to pick them up. You would not be introduced to work as a structural engineer slowly or in a very controlled way. You would become involved with projects at an early stage and work alongside Peter. There was something of a 'sink or swim' attitude. If you felt you were sinking, Peter was always there to help, although this happened relatively rarely. He chose his young team so that they would be resilient and self-sufficient from the very beginning. Rapidly we were asked to come up with ideas and concepts for designs. Prior experience was not a pre-requisite, possibly even the contrary. Peter was particularly fond of the early Gothic cathedrals, which had been realized by people who were discovering how to build them for the first time. He believed in the benefits of 'the first time'. He liked people with no preconceived ideas.

Early on in Arup, I worked with him on a large holotrame sculpture in Place d'Italie in Paris and he took me to meet the artist, look at the early models, in order to understand the artist's desires and start to think how we might go about making the piece. He was clearly encouraging me to work in the way he liked to work, in the architect's or artist's office. He would often involve me from the start, offering me the chance to be present in the earliest days, not keeping it to himself, but inviting me to participate in meetings in a very open way. Peter was at the time travelling enormously and, although he would try to make time for all of us in the office, the best times you had with him were when you were travelling together. It was possible then to talk about projects, about ideas. Those moments with Peter were really precious.

Then we would come back to London and we would need to start thinking and discussing concepts and solutions. Surprise was important to him. He liked to play tricks with perception, so that the viewer did not quite understand how the structure worked. There would be apparent instability so that people would ask themselves how it was all hanging together. Yet the concepts would always be underpinned by sound and clear engineering principles. The apparent instability was one of his ways of attracting attention to the structure. Generally the work we did together relied heavily on structural analysis, because the structures and their geometry were complex and, without the assistance of computer modelling and mathematics, it could not be predicted how they would behave. The calculations were part of the thinking. Colleagues and myself would carry out some initial modelling and simulations, and then resume the conversation with Peter.

The role of the conversation was important to Peter. He often explained to me that one of the things he liked about working in France was that concepts would be discussed early on, but not committed to drawings immediately. He felt that drawing would have the effect of freezing the ideas too quickly, not giving him enough space to introduce new notions of materials and manufacturing.

He was especially interested in manufacturing. When new techniques became available for the materials he used, he would wish to apply them in the next project. For example, he interrupted the process of fabrication of rolled-steel sections in order to give an unexpected effect to the lampposts at Esch sur Lazette in Luxembourg. He knew that he could in this way arrive at a shape that would attract the eye and make people question what it was they were seeing.

The ideas would develop over a period of several weeks through conversations with the project team, and also those he met at the same time on other projects. This organic process of thinking seemed very natural. It seemed like the thing you were supposed to do if you were an engineer: to think about the context, the project, and integrate what you knew of science, mathematics, the tactile aspects of materials, and manufacturing techniques, with ideas.

For example, Peter initiated the stone lattice at the Seville World Exposition 1992 because of his awareness of advances in stone cutting in Spain. He was a collector of manufacturing knowledge and he liked to play with it. He often felt that industrial manufacturing could be alienating rather than inviting. He wanted to make *les traces de la main* apparent in his structures, not only in relation to the making but also in relation to the sense of touch. This preoccupation began with the famous gerberettes of the Centre Pompidou in Paris. His interest in stone began with his time in Spain, where he not only witnessed progress in the precision of stone cutting but also the ruins of a church where the only elements that remained standing were the structural stone arches. This coincided with the beginning of several projects, investigating the capacity of stone: from the traditional hand-carved masonry of the Full-Moon Theatre, to the beautifully translucent marble façade of Lille Cathedral, via the vertiginous stone and steel arches fronting the Pavilion of the Future at the Seville World Exposition 1992. This free-standing filigree screen made a daring use of stone as a structural material that Peter felt could have as lively a future as steel, concrete and textiles. The Seville façade also illustrated his love for light tensile structures and his research in using a repetition of light elements to create almost virtual surfaces within the structural space. This borrowed in no small way from the Gothic cathedrals that Peter loved so much.

At this time of his career, architects and clients would come to him in search of an idea. However, Peter produced his best works with strong architects, where two very strong minds would exchange ideas and in collaboration progress a design. Architecture requires a careful balancing of criteria and disciplines to avoid any one aspect overtaking the design. When Peter was asked to come up with a total solution, the result could be structurally flamboyant. After all, as he insisted, Peter was a structural engineer, not an architect.

Engineers have often thought that Peter was particularly lucky with the commissions he was given. Late in his career people did come to Peter with extraordinary projects, but for the most part it was Peter who made his own luck. He would use any opportunity to achieve something special. Ideas would flow between projects. Projects and encounters would cross-feed. He was there to make every project count. He also worked when architecture was inspired by engineering and wanted to celebrate it, to expose it. The Centre Pompidou in Paris may even be at the origin of this inspiration.

None of his projects were simple. They had all the difficulties of construction projects and more. When you wish to do something special, you have to convince a lot more people along the way. He had that ability to take people with him. It is so easy to kill an idea; there are so many doubters, so many Iagos as he described them in *An Engineer Imagines*. He was able to make projects happen in a manner that appeared almost effortless, although anyone involved in the construction industry knows that it is anything but effortless. He had huge communication skills, not just the design skills he is renowned for. He was most persuasive: walking on uncertain ground and persuading others that they too could do it. He did this in a manner that was never coercive. You never felt you had been pushed into a corner. With his clarity of thinking, it seemed effortless, it seemed normal.

Since that time, he is there in almost every project I have done. There is a quote I often refer to, when I am starting a project or facing a difficult question. I call it the 'courage quote' and Peter's words have accompanied me all these years.

> If we go back and examine this innovative façade and its use of stone, we find that at each stage the spur to proceed was created by something that already existed. Each step was prompted by something similar that could be used as a guide. Innovation here was the development of existing ideas and the belief that they were relevant and applicable in the structure we were exploring.
>
> Perhaps the missing ingredient is courage. The courage you need is the courage to start. Once launched, then each step can evolve naturally. Each step requires careful examination. The courage to start and an unshakeable belief in one's ability to solve the new problems that will arise in the development are essential. It is important to emphasize here that the team should have at least three or four members capable of contributing at every stage of the development. Every stage of the design should be subject to detailed scrutiny by engineers who feel themselves to be sharing in the responsibility. Nothing must be left to chance. Others not so closely involved must also be asked to review the project to question the assumptions and demand explanations.

There are at least three structures that would not be what they are if, as a key engineer in their construction, I had not worked with Peter. One of his main influences is a continuing

99

Millennium Bridge
(Norman Foster),
London 2000.

concern for the integration of architecture with engineering. A particularly good example of this concern is the work I did on London's Millennium Bridge with Norman Foster: integrating the non-structural with the structural and making the concept happen. The concept was that people would feel as if they were walking on wire when crossing the river. This was achieved by the strong horizontality of the suspension bridge. At the southern end of the bridge, the bridge deck, arriving at the south bank, separates and there is a gap in the middle for the exit ramp. As the bridge is suspended from the main cables, you might wonder what is happening at that point where you are suspended only from one side. This is indeed quite unusual and most people will probably not notice, because we were able to find a solution in the continuity of the rest of the deck. There was considerable discussion about that element of the bridge. Some members of the team suggested that we use supporting columns. However, for me it was an absolute impossibility to allow that, because we would have failed in what we were supposed to do: *suspend* the bridge from one side of the river to the other; not stop half way and place it on columns. We must keep the truth of the idea. I was definitely thinking about Peter at that time. The solution to this is visible under the bridge deck. The structural system relies on torsion. Torsion is not something that engineers use very often to make things stand up. They generally prefer to rely on a more direct way of supporting gravity. Torsion is something that is largely ignored, but it is something that Peter was using all the time. That was one of his engineering tricks: to use the capacity available in torsion to make things stand up, things that look as if they should not. I had used this with him in the Lille TGV Station roof structure. I used it again with the Millennium Bridge.

Another project where Peter was strongly present is Pierres Vives in Montpellier designed by Zaha Hadid. Here the influence is not as visible as in the Millennium Bridge. Zaha knew Peter and he had helped her by giving her confidence early on that some of the ideas she wished to achieve could happen. The Montpellier project is a project essentially in concrete, a material not often used by Peter. Yet there is the same desire not to allow the structure to betray the architectural concept but to serve the architecture and work in harmony with the building functions and building envelope, with its alternance of voids and solid blocks. One of the key objectives of the structural design was to achieve an impression of lightness, of effortless levitation of the solid blocks. This provides surprise and an appearance of lightness that I hope Peter would have appreciated. I owe to him this desire to find a structural solution that appears, however heroic, to be almost effortless.

The project where most often I thought of Peter is the construction of the Centre Pompidou-Metz. The competition took place around 2004, twelve years after Peter's death. As the engineer for this, the second Centre Pompidou, I was keenly aware of an historical thread between my work and his. The project clearly shows how architecture had moved on and away from its preoccupations when Peter was designing Beaubourg in the 1970s. Metz was a project where the engineering challenge was immense but was without any intention to celebrate the fact. It was a project where even starting required courage.

Pierres Vives interior (Zaha Hadid), Montpellier 2012.

Pierres Vives atrium, Montpellier 2012.

There are two quotations from Peter that I always return to: the 'courage quote' and also the 'hound quote' found at the end of *An Engineer Imagines*. It is about following the idea like a hound with its nose to the ground: following what your analysis is telling you and what the idea is telling you, and pushing on further to develop it. I go back often to those words because they are the source of what I do.

> When people come to buy surprise I have no idea what I'm going to give them either. It's not like I am going out of my way to surprise them, I'm actually quite often surprised myself by what the outcome is because I am a bit like a hound following a fox; I'm following something really close to the ground and I can't actually see where it's going. I've got my nose to the ground to make sure I am following it properly.

When you begin a roof timber structure like that at Metz you need courage and you need an extraordinary amount of confidence that you will be able to solve the problems. It is all about a method, a way of working, where the initial structural concept will tell you what it needs. Unusual concepts are rare for engineers and I am very lucky to have been able to work with some amazing structures over the years. It is never obvious that you will find a solution but you must listen to the idea and what it is telling you. And you listen to what the analysis is telling you, and you follow the thread, the scent. You listen to what the materials and the methods of construction are telling you. There is a certain amount of intuition, trying to understand how things are moving, how things are behaving. And then the project takes you beyond where you imagined you could go and you find the surprise and delight that Peter taught me to seek, twenty years ago.

**ABOVE**
Centre Pompidou-
Metz atrium.

**RIGHT**
Centre Pompidou-
Metz roof and
interior.

Marble Curtain (Studio/Gang), Chicago 2012.

# Peter Heppel

PETER TAUGHT US to listen – to our architects and building occupants, to our materials and the flow of forces, to our Iago-like contractors and their underrated craft-workers. And that to listen is more than to hear: it is to look beyond the words, the appearance and the habits, to match what is really possible to what is really needed. Peter taught us to trust in logic, to construct our justification in the face of precedent. Peter taught us that innovation doesn't take bravery if you do your homework: it becomes natural. Peter taught us to make sure that our calculation methods free us rather than limit us. Advanced calculation takes clever software. Design freedom takes software that does what you dream of doing, not just what you have done.

Twenty years later, our textile design software is delivering this freedom from precedent – and is freely available as open-source so that everyone can use it and add to it. This has been Peter's legacy to us: design freedom via calculation. It has enabled a few modest results: a demountable structure for NASA stressed twenty times higher than any architectural textile, some near-perfect sails for the America's Cup, a marble jigsaw as a tensile structure and the extraordinary dynamic wind sculptures of the artist Janet Echelman.

**ABOVE**
Passerella Olimpico
(Hugh Dutton), Turin
2006.

**LEFT**
Islamic Art Pavilion
(Mario Bellini),
Louvre, Paris 2012.

# Hugh Dutton

I MET PETER in 1981, at the moment RFR began and the La Villette Science Museum project was starting. I had just finished my studies at the Architectural Association and had decided that my training as an architect lacked a fundamental ingredient: knowing how to build. I followed Peter to Paris, and worked with him on the La Villette greenhouses, where we developed the articulated bolt-and-cable-truss system together with Francis and Ritchie. He asked me to write with him the book *Structural Glass* to tell the story of our approach to design. It has become today the reference for students and young professionals, as he wished it to be, and the initial French text has been translated into English, Korean, Italian and Chinese.

As a young architect I grew up in his world of engineering design and we discussed often the common ground between engineering, architecture, and sculpture and the muddling of those *métiers* into one of just designing. I recall when we were translating *Structural Glass*, the significance of 'design' was a problem because it means something very different in French, where it has a connotation of style.

In my recent work I still carry Peter and these discussions with me. He taught me lessons of geometry, about steel, glass, timber, stone and light. About pushing the limits in industry. About asking simple questions.

The Passerella Olimpico in Turin, Italy, began as a conversation about one Peter was planning in Spain with Richard Rogers, where the deck-suspension cables stabilize the funicular-arch shape.

The Louvre Islamic Art Pavilion where my firm HDA provided technical assistance, engineering and detailing for Mario Bellini and Rudy Ricciotti's idea of a light filtering veil proposing dancing columns, that supporti an intricate parametrically optimized space frame, clad in low iron glass and expanded metal meshes. It is fitting that this autumn the pavilion is opened marking the twenty years since he left us. Through it he is still contributing to the Louvre, as he did for the sculpture courtyard glass roofs, and the inverted pyramid.

The west window of Lille Cathedral is a fundmental trace. Peter's last work, in which he gave poetry to stone in light.

New façade, Cathédrale Notre-Dame de la Treille (Pierre-Louis Carlier with L. Kinjo), Lille 1991.

Cathédrale Notre-Dame de la Treille interior, Lille 1991.

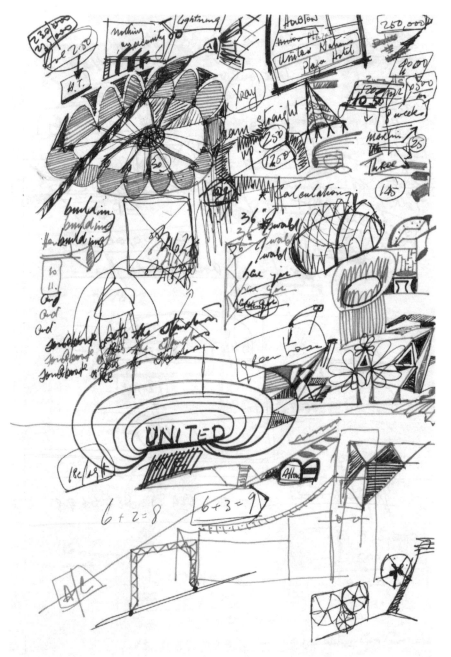

Repeated doodles: 'Building ... I would ... have you ... Someone sets the standard'; in red, green and blue; 'UNITED'; 6+2=8, 6+3=9 (boxed). Peter Rice Notebook, February – April 1982.

## 11

# On first looking into Rice's engineering notebooks

## J. Philip O'Kane

The forty-seven Rice notebooks run from January 1980 to April 1991. The originals are Windsor & Newton black and white sketchbooks containing ninety-four leaves of A4 bond paper perforated down the spine for easy removal. Coloured boards in either wine or black enclose each sketchbook. Each is labelled on the spine with the start and end date of the entries; some dates are not known. The Rice family added these labels to the notebooks following their collection after Peter's death. When placed on a timeline, the labels cover roughly 70 per cent of the period 1980 to 1991.

Each notebook was the informal *vade mecum* of Peter Rice during his work day in London, Paris or Genoa. The entries follow no set pattern; there is no index to each notebook. A wavy line, a new page, or a change of ink, separates one entry from another. The word 'meeting' occurs now and then, sometimes with a list of names, business cards stapled to the page, Post-its, a date, and occasionally a place. We look in vain for project code numbers beloved of company accountants, especially the code number for 'reading and thinking not specific to costed jobs', the catalyst for new beginnings. Echoes from copybooks at school, or notebooks from university, are beyond our hearing.

There are many instructions to himself, 'Phone Renzo [Piano]', outlines of talks to be given somewhere not named, notes for interviews or articles on his work, phone numbers of colleagues in the UK, France, Italy, USA, and delightful requests in the handwriting of his daughters for books they needed in their studies.

The Rice notebooks are replete with sketches. The design of a physical object by artisans, architects, engineers, and inventors, starts with a sketch.[1] The form, shape, size, texture, and appearance, of designed objects are the product of non-verbal modes of thought and decision by the designer. They are contingent on scientific laws, facts and data, but are not determined by science. Many of the Rice sketches are the outward expression of what he imagined[2] in his mind's eye[3] in response to a client architect, or artist, asking him questions, demanding solutions: Can my design be built? Will it 'work'? What changes of form, material, structural action, lighting … in minute detail … will better achieve my goals as an architect, as an artist, and satisfy our patrons?

The Rice sketches are not the sketches of an artist-engineer of the French Ecole des Ponts et Chausées,[4] or of the English industrial revolution,[5] or of the Italian *Rinascimento*.[6] There are no perspective views, no orthographic projections, no exploded views, no meticulous exploration of the anatomy of machine or body, no light and shadow, no colour washes, no military devices for attack and defence, no swirling wind or water, no hatching with the left hand, nor mirrored annotation.

The late historian-engineer, Eugene S. Ferguson,[7] distinguished between three kinds of sketches by engineers: the *thinking* sketch, the *talking* sketch, and the *prescriptive* sketch.

The purpose of the *thinking* sketch[8] is to focus and guide private non-verbal thinking.

The *talking* sketch is the most important medium of communication, firstly, among engineers (and architects) as designers; secondly, between engineers and draughtsmen, in the

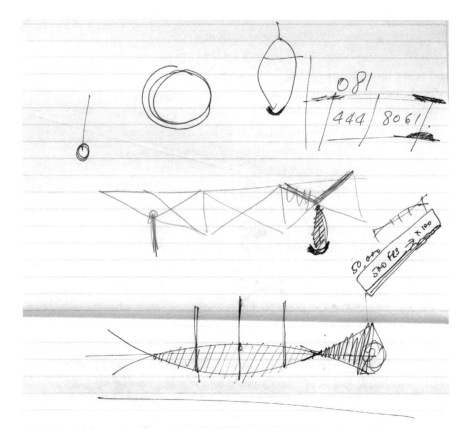

An bhfuil áthas ort anois

An bfuil átas ort anois        *oṫ. anois*

on will áwhass urth anish

                              Slante war.

'Are you happy now?' in Irish: Peter explains, perhaps to one of his children, that the letter *h* is an aspirant providing a phonetic rendering in English, Peter Rice Notebook: September – November 1981.

Two trusses, the second a talking sketch in ink. Perhaps a 'eureka' moment for the architect showing the Rice cable truss, with the rough cost of 100 cable trusses, to support a vertical wall of glass carried on circular columns, with reference to the *Façades Bioclimatiques* at La Villette. Peter Rice Notebook: inserted page at the end, September – November 1981.

clarification of details in prescriptive sketches that guide them; and thirdly, when engineers solicit the views of artisans in fabrication shops before making a prototype.

The *prescriptive* sketch directs the draughtsman or woman, whether she is assisted by a computer or not, in the making of a finished printed drawing.[9] The printed drawing[10] is an instrument of human control: a precise instruction to the operatives and artisans in a factory, fabrication shop or building site on what is to be made and how it is to be made.

The Rice notebooks contain private *thinking* sketches and social *talking* sketches.[11] Missing pages may have contained *prescriptive* sketches handed to a draughtsman. While Rice's artistry is not of the Vincian kind, we recognize his individual style in the sketches from notebook to notebook.[12]

We also find sketches of parts of architectural structures and of the forces acting on and in them. 'Back of an envelope'[13] calculations of forces in equilibrium often accompany the sketches, but not always. His design team could attend to the more detailed analysis of forces and displacements, cost, performance and safety, recording the results in formal project notebooks of engineering calculations.

The most opaque of all the entries in the notebooks are the doodles that now and then burst out of the page expressing emotion, perhaps anxiety, when a project is not running to plan, or simply the distraction of a client speaking far too fast in Italian, or French.

Rice tells us what he meant by *design as creative imagining* in his autobiography.[14] He describes the moment of inspiration following days of searching, when the fully formed, one-and-only solution suddenly appears in his mind's eye: on waking from sleep in the case of the double gerberette beam of Beaubourg; and while distracted by another project in the case of the structure of the Lloyds Building. These non-verbal solutions were driven upwards by his will from his prepared subconscious mind.

The search for evidence of such epiphanies in the notebooks demands a complete knowledge of the context in which they were written and drawn. This is not an easy task.[15] There are six illustrative sketches in the autobiography.[16] None are taken from the existing notebooks. The architect André Brown, in his overview[17] of Rice's work, uses illustrative sketches from the notebooks, and from other sources, which are acknowledged. These other sources should be added to the Rice digital archive.

Rice spoke of himself as an engineering strategist. His notebooks show him in action, and record his passion for building physics and the novel use of materials in the service of architecture. The electronic copy of the notebooks makes possible their systematic examination as cultural artefacts in the different disciplines of art and architectural history,[18] science and technology studies,[19] professional engineering[20] and architectural studies. The extensive footnotes in this short essay are signposts – to Darien – for the academically brave as they travel these paths in search of Peter Rice and his engineering.[21]

*Go mba fada buan sibh!*

# NOTES

[1] J. Christopher Jones in his book *Design Methods: Seeds of Human Futures* (John Wiley & Sons, London, 1970) explains the transition over decades from traditional craft methods to 'design by drawing' in terms of *division of labour, greater size and complexity,* and *economies of scale.* Furthermore, 'The effect of concentrating the geometric aspects of manufacture in a drawing is to give the designer a much greater "perceptual span" than the craftsman had. The designer can (by use of a drawing) see and manipulate the design as a whole and is not prevented, either by partial knowledge or by the high cost of altering the product itself, from making fairly drastic changes in design.'

[2] Peter Rice, *An Engineer Imagines* (Artemis, London, Zurich, Munich, 1994).

[3] Eugene S. Ferguson, *Engineering and the Mind's Eye* (The MIT Press, Cambridge, Massachusetts, 1992).

⁴ Antoine Picon and Michel Yvon. *L'ingénieur Artiste: Dessins Anciens de l'Ecole des Ponts et Chaussées* (Presses de l'Ecole Nationale des Ponts et Chaussées, Paris, 1989).

⁵ Ken Baynes and Francis Pugh, *The Art of the Engineer* (Lutterworth Press, Guildford, England, 1987). Examples of Victorian engineers' notebooks appear on pp. 109–10, pp. 155–57.

⁶ The late art-historian Gustina Scaglia 'correlated the drawings of ten engineers' notebooks to show the exchange of information among Renaissance engineers. Scaglia noted the repetition of cranes and other machines for lifting and moving the heavy materials used in monumental buildings … Lifting devices were but one of several preoccupations … Another was military machines … Other subjects of wide interest were the raising of water for public and private fountains and the design of water-powered flour mills, sawmills, and other industrial units.' See her 'Drawings of Machines for Architecture from the Early Quattrocento in Italy', *Journal of the Society of Architectural Historians*, vol. 25, no. 2 (May 1966). The quotations are from pp. 64–6 and p. 207 of Eugene S. Ferguson *op. cit. ante*.

⁷ Eugene S. Ferguson *op. cit. ante*, pp. 96–7. See also the work of the sociologist Kathryn Henderson, 'Flexible Sketches and Inflexible Data Bases: Visual Communication, Conscription Devices, and Boundary Objects in Design Engineering', *Science Technology Human Values*, vol. 16, no. 4 (October 1991), pp. 448–73. Kathryn Henderson, On Line and On Paper: Visual Representations, Visual Culture and Computer Graphics in *Design Engineering* (MIT Press, Inside Technology Series, January 1999).

⁸ For a study of Leonardo's thinking while sketching, see Bert S. Hall and Ian Bates, 'Leonardo, the Chiaravalle Clock and Epicyclic Gearing: A Reply to Antonio Simoni', *Antiquarian Horology*, vol. 9 (September 1976), pp. 910–17. Quoted in Ferguson *op. cit. ante*, pp. 99, 232.

⁹ Baynes and Pugh present a basic typology of drawings that 'appears to have emerged early in the development of the engineering industry and then to have continued through to the present day'. Their categories are *designers' drawings* frequently found as sketches in the personal notebooks of senior engineers, *project drawings* showing proposals in broad outline and produced according to accepted rules and conventions, *production drawings* covering every detail of the product to be manufactured, *presentation and maintenance drawings* made after the product has been finished, and *technical illustrations* for technical or popularizing books, or nowadays, for sales and marketing. *Op. cit. ante*, pp. 14–15.

¹⁰ Private *thinking* and social *talking* sketches are not confined to notebooks. They may also appear on printed drawings.

¹¹ 'Bruce Archer [of the Royal College of Art] has suggested that designers operate in a way that is analogous to a movie camera, changing focus and definition from one part of the design to another, allowing the various parts to affect one another until sharp definition is achieved throughout. Engineers' notebooks tend to confirm this theory.' Quoted by Baynes and Pugh, *op. cit. ante*, pp. 14, 237.

¹² Reese V. Jenkins, 'Elements of Style: Continuities in Edison's Thinking', in *Bridge to the Future: A Centennial Celebration of the Brooklyn Bridge*, ed. M. Latimer et al (New York, 1984) and the related papers on design by Robert M. Vogel and Edwin T. Layton Jr., quoted in Ferguson, *op. cit. ante*, pp. 26, 199. The Edison notebooks are discussed in R. Jenkins et al., *The Papers of Thomas A. Edison* (Baltimore, 1989), quoted in Ferguson, *op. cit. ante*, p. 213.

¹³ Henry Petroski, 'On the Backs of Envelopes', *American Scientist* (January–February 1991).

¹⁴ *An Engineer Imagines*, p. 79.

¹⁵ A detailed chronology of the Rice buildings and projects, in much greater detail than that in the autobiography, is a priority. For example, whereas the chronology gives 1991 as the date for the Pyramide Inversée, Grand Louvre, a sketch of an inverted pyramid first appears in the notebook for Sept–Oct 1988. Apparently, Rice was thinking about the project almost three years before the contract began.

¹⁶ On p. 88 (Menil Building), p. 101 (Nuage structure), p. 120 (Pavilion of the Future), p. 150 (Full-Moon Theatre), p. 197 (Inverted Pyramid), and a supplementary page at the end of the first edition.

¹⁷ André Brown, *Peter Rice: The Engineer's Contribution to Contemporary Architecture* (ICE Publishing, London, 2001).

¹⁸ Gustina Scaglia , 'Typology of Leonardo da Vinci's Machine Drawings and Sketches', in *Leonardo da Vinci, Engineer and Architect*, P. Galluzzi and J. Guillaume (eds.) (Montreal Museum of Fine Arts, Montreal, 1987). Antoine Picon, *Architectes et Ingénieurs au Siècle des Lumières* (Parenthèses, Marseille, 1988), translated by Martin Thom as *Architects and Engineers in the Age of Enlightenment* (Cambridge University Press, 2009).

¹⁹ See for example: Bruno Latour, *Aramis ou l'Amour des Techniques* (La Découverte, Paris, 1992), translated by Catherine Porter as *Aramis, or the Love of Technology* (Harvard University Press, 1996). Bruno Latour,

*Science in Action: How to Follow Scientists and Engineers Through Society* (Harvard University Press, 1987).

20 Antoine Picon, *L'Invention de l'Ingénieur Moderne – L'Ecole des Ponts et Chaussées* 1747 – 1851 (Presses de l'Ecole Nationale des Ponts et Chaussées, Paris, 1992). Antoine Picon (sous sa direction), *L'Art de l'Ingénieur – Constructeur, Entrepreneur, Inventeur* (Centre Georges Pompidou, Paris, 1997).

21 Years of reflection by Rice, from his architectural apprenticeship under Jørn Utzen in Sydney to the use of structural glass at La Villette, lie behind his 'Engineering Method: Process, Prediction and Hierarchy', which is described in detail in his book with Hugh Dutton *Le Verre Structurel* (Editions du Moniteur, Paris, 1990). The *postface* at the end of the book, describing more recent projects, was expanded for the second edition and translated into many other languages, including English.

# TEXT ILLUSTRATION CREDITS

*Listed by page number*

# Select projects

1957 – Sydney Opera House, Sydney

1971 – Centre Pompidou, Paris

1971 – Conference Centre, Mecca

1978 – Fleetguard, Quimper

1978 – Lloyd's of London Redevelopment

1978 – Patscentre, Princeton

1980 – Fabric roof canopy,
      Schlumberger Headquarters, Montrouge

1981 – Glass façades and central reception area roof, La Villette, Paris

1981 – IBM Mobile Pavilion

1981 – Menil Collection museum, Houston

1981 – Stansted Airport Terminal Building

1985 – Lord's Mound Stand, London

1985 – Design of steel structure for glass roof of courtyards, Grand Louvre, Paris

1986 – Canopies, Parc de la Villette, Paris

1986 – San Nicola football stadium, Bari

1986 – Nuage Léger, Tête Défense, Paris

1986 – Passerelle Lintas, Paris

1987 – Parc Citroën Cévennes, Greenhouses, Paris

1988 – Façade of the BPOA, Rennes

1988 – Glazed Roof Canopy, BusRail Station, Chur

1988 – Kansai International Airport

1988 – La Grande Nef, Tête Défense, Paris

1988 – Les Tours de la Liberté, Paris

1988 – TGV/RER Charles de Gaulle, Roissy

1988 – Full-Moon Theatre, Mas de Gourgoubès

1988 – Usine Centre, St Herblain

1989 – BIGO Tent, Genoa

1989 – L'Oréal Factory, Aulnay

1989 – Pavilion of the Future, Seville World Exposition 1992

1989 – Queen's Stand, Epsom Racecourse, Surrey

1989 – Research project on Spiders' Webs

1989 – Sloping glazed façade and roof, Shell, Rueil Malmaison

1989 – Toronto Opera House

1990 – Canopy and façades for CNIT, Paris

1990 – Chiesa Padre Pio church, St Giovanni Rotondo

1990 – Study for Structure of Roof, Groningen Museum

1991 – Atrium glazing, 50 Avenue Montaigne, Paris

1991 – Brau&Brunnen Tower, Berlin

1991 – Glass façades, Renault Technocentre, Guyancourt

1991 – Japan Bridge, La Défense, Paris

1991 – Lamppost, Esch sur Alzette

1991 – Pyramide Inversée, Grand Louvre, Paris

1991 – Roof Design, TGV Station, Lille

1991 – West Window, Cathédrale Notre Dame de la Treille, Lille

121

122

Conference Centre, Mecca 1971. Photo: Arup

Patscentre, Princeton 1978. Photo: Otto Baitz

Fabric roof canopy, Schlumberger Headquarters, Montrouge 1980. Photo: Harry Sowden

Stansted Airport Terminal Building 1981. Photo: Ken Kirkwood

Glass façades and central reception area roof,
La Villette 1981. Photo: Martin Charles

Lord's Mound Stand, London 1985.
Photo: Richard Bryant

Canopies, Parc de la Villette 1986. Photo: RFR

San Nicola Football Stadium, Bari 1986.
Photo: Arup

Nuage Léger, Tête Défense 1986.
Photo: John Edward Linden

Glazed Roof Canopy, BusRail Station, Chur 1988. Photo: RFR

Façade of the BPOA, Rennes 1988. Photo: RFR / ADAGP

La Grande Nef, Tête Défense, Paris 1988.
Photo: RFR / ADAGP

Kansai International Airport 1988. Photo: Y. Kinumaki

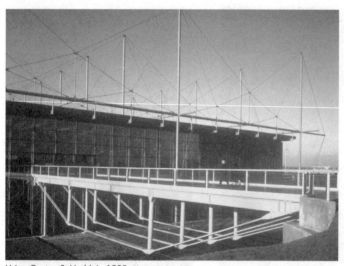

Usine Center, St Herblain 1988. Photo: Richard Bryant

BIGO Tent, Genoa 1989. Photo: Alistair Lenczner

Les Tours de la Liberté, Paris 1988. Photo: RFR

Seville World Exposition, Seville 1989.
Photo: Fernando Alda

Canopy and Façades for CNIT, Paris 1990. Photo: RFR

Japan Bridge, La Défense 1991. Photo: Kate Purver

Glass façades, Renault Technocentre, Guyancourt 1991. Photo: Alistair Lenczner

Grande Pyramide Inversée, 1991. Photo: Sophie Le Bourva

# Select publications

## WORKS BY PETER RICE

P. Rice (1971), 'Notes on the Design of Cable Roofs', *Arup Journal*, vol. 6, no. 4, pp. 6–10.

E. F. Happold and P. Rice (1973), 'Introduction', *Arup Journal*, Centre Beaubourg special issue, vol. 8, no. 2, June, pp. 2–3.

P. Rice and L. Grut (1975), 'Main Structural Framework of the Beaubourg Centre', Paris, *Acier Stahl Steel*, vol. 40, no. 9, September, pp. 297–309.

P. Rice and R. Peirce (1976), 'The Barrettes of Centre Georges Pompidou', South African Institution of Civil Engineers, Fifth Quinquennial Regional Convention, Stellenbosch University, 28–30 September (Innovations in Civil Engineering conference paper).

P. Rice and A. Day (1977), 'Lagoon Barriers at Venice', *Arup Journal*, vol. 12, no. 2, pp. 21–22.

P. Rice (1977), 'Materials in Use: Fire Protection and Maintenance at the Centre Pompidou', *RIBA Journal*, vol. 84, no. 11, November, pp. 476–477.

P. B. Ahm, F. G. Clarke, E. L. Grut and P. Rice (1979, 1980), 'Design and Construction of the Centre National d'Art et de Culture Georges Pompidou', *ICE Proceedings*, part 1, no. 66, pp. 557–93 (November 1979), part 1, no. 68, pp. 499–505 (August 1980).

P. Rice (1980), 'The Structural and Geometric Characteristics of Lightweight Structures', Ove Arup Partnership: Arup Partnerships' Seminar: Lightweight Structures, March, 8 pages.

P. Rice (1980), 'Lightwieght Structures: Introduction', *Arup Journal*, vol. 15, no. 3, October, pp. 2–5.

P. Rice (1981), 'Long Spans and Soft Skins', *Consulting Engineer*, vol. 45, no. 7, pp. 10–12.

P. Rice, T. Barker, A. Guthrie and N. Noble (1983), 'The Menil Collection, Houston Texas', *Arup Journal*, vol. 18, no. 1, pp. 2–7.

J. Young, P. Rice, J. Thornton (1984), 'Design for Better Assembly: (5) Case Study: Rogers' and Arup's', *The Architects' Journal*, vol. 180, no. 36, 5 September, pp. 87–94.

A. A. Tassel and P. Rice (1985), 'Master of the hi-tech Style. Britain's Peter Rice', *SA Construction World*, April, pp. 54–61.

P. Rice (1986), 'Rogers Revolution', *Building Design*, no. 807, 10 October, pp. 32–3.

P. Rice and J. A. Thornton (1986), 'Lloyd's Redevelopment', *Structural Engineer*, vol. 64A, no. 10, October, pp. 265–81.

A. Day, T. Haslett, T. Carfrae and P. Rice (1986), 'Buckling and Non-linear Behaviour of Space Frames', International Conference on Lightweight Structures in Architecture, Sydney, no. 1, August (LSA 86), pp. 775–82.

P. Rice (1987), 'Il Punto di Vista di Peter Rice' ('An Engineer's View'), *L'Arca*, no. 5, April, pp. 70–5.

P. Rice (1987), 'Menil Collection museum Roof: Evolving the Form', *Arup Journal*, vol. 22, no. 2, Summer, pp. 2–5.

P. Rice (1987), 'The Controlled Energy of Renzo Piano', *Renzo Piano: The Process of Architecture*, exhibition catalogue, 1987 (9H Gallery, London).

P. Rice, J.A. Thornton, A. Lenczner (1988), 'Cable-Stayed Roofs for Shopping Centres at Nantes and Epone', *Structural Engineering Review*, no. 1, pp. 133–40.

Interview with Peter Rice, *Le Moniteur*, no. 4453, 31 March 1989, pp. 46–7.

P. Rice (1989), 'A Celebration of the Life and Work of Ove Arup', *RSA Journal*, June, pp. 425–37, reprinted in *Arup Journal*, vol. 25, no. 1, Spring 1990, pp. 43–7.

P. Rice (1989), 'Building as Craft, Building as Industry', *Guggenheim Museum Proceedings*, New York, pp. 87–9.

P. Rice (1990) 'Constructive Intelligence', *Arch +*, no. 102, January, pp. 37-52.

C. Gabato and P. Rice (1990), 'Bari', *Architecktur Aktuell*, vol. 24, no. 139, October, pp. 82–85.

P. Rice (1990), 'Unstable Structures', *Columbia Documents of Architecture and Theory*, vol. 1 (Rizzoli, New York), pp. 71–90.

P. Rice and H. Dutton (1990), *Le Verre Structurel* (Editions du Moniteur, Paris); trans. Martine Erussard, *Structural Glass*, 1996.

P. Rice, A. Lenczner, T. Carfrae, and A. Sedgwick (1990), 'The San Nicola Stadium, Bari', *Arup Journal*, vol. 25, no. 3, Autumn, pp. 3–8.

P. Rice, A. Lenczner and T. Carfrae (1991), 'The San Nicola Stadium, Bari', *Steel Construction Today*, vol. 5, no. 4, July, pp. 157–60.

P. Rice (1991), 'Practice and Europe', *The Structural Engineer*, vol. 69, no. 23, 3 December, pp. 400–1.

P. Rice (1991), 'Architecture Now, Arcam Pocket', chapter: 'Peter Rice – Great Britain'. *Architectura & Natura*, pp 127–8.

P. Rice (1991), 'Materials and Design Using Timber as a Model', International Timber Engineering Conference, London.

P. Rice (1991), 'Menil Collection Museum Roof: Evolving the Form', *Offramp*, vol. 1, no. 4, pp. 117–19.

P. Rice (1992), 'Dilemma of Technology' in A. Tzonis and L. Lefaivre, *Architecture in Europe since 1968: Memory and Intervention* (Thames & Hudson, London), pp 36–41.

P. Rice (1992), Speech at 1992 RIBA Gold Medal Presentation, *RIBA Journal*, September.

RIBA (1992), *Exploring Materials: the work of Peter Rice* (RIBA Gallery, London).

P. Rice (1994), *An Engineer Imagines* (Artemis, London, Zurich, Munich).

# Notes on contributors

HENRY BARDSLEY worked with Peter Rice at Arup and RFR on design
and analysis of structures and surfaces. President of RFR from 1993 to
2006. Worked on the octagonal tower in Luxembourg and the lenticular
pectinate footbridge across the Seine. Civil engineer of Imperial College,
he is a recipient of the Gold Medal of the Institution of Civil Engineers.

KEVIN BARRY, a graduate of UCD and Cambridge University, Professor
Emeritus, School of Humanities, NUI Galway, has published widely on
literature and the arts during the eighteenth century, and on modern Irish
literature.

BARBARA CAMPBELL-LANGE is an architect and teacher. She
studied at the Bartlett UCL, the Architectural Association, Cooper Union
and Cambridge. She is Academic Coordinator of the Architectural
Association.

ED CLARK M.Eng. C.Eng. MI.Struct.E. MICE is a Director of Arup in
London He studied engineering at Leeds University and joined Arup in
1996. Key projects have included the Selfridges building in Birmingham
and the Serpentine Gallery Summer Pavilions. In 2011 he was awarded the
IABSE Milne Medal for excellence in the field of structural design.

HUGH DUTTON graduated from Architectural Association in London,
after preliminary training at the University of Waterloo in Ontario,
Canada. He began his professional career with Peter Rice and founded in
1995 Hugh Dutton Associates, a specialist design company based in Paris,
working in collaboration with leading architects.

MARTIN FRANCIS, a founding partner and shareholder in RFR, is a
designer and naval architect who maintains collaboration with Frank
Stella in addition to a number of projects in architecture and yacht design.

JONATHAN GLANCEY is a writer and broadcaster. He was Architecture and Design correspondent of *The Guardian* from 1997 to 2012, and Architecture and Design editor of *The Independent* from 1987 to 1997.

JENNIFER GREITSCHUS Ph.D. founded Phase 2 exhibitions at Arup in 2008 to explore the intersection of art and culture with engineering and other disciplines. Before joining Arup she worked at the Museum of Modern Art, Frankfurt-am-Main, the South Bank Centre, London and Documenta XI, Kassel.

PETER HEPPEL, aeronautical engineer, worked with Peter Rice at Arup until 1992. He researches and designs soft structures with a focus on the characteristics and behaviours of textile and wind.

SOPHIE LE BOURVA is an Associate Director in the UK–MEA Division in Arup. A graduate of the Ecole Polytechnique, the Ecole Nationale des Ponts et Chaussées, the Ecole d'Architecture Paris-La-Seine and Cambridge University, her projects include Lille TGV station, the London Millennium Footbridge, Pierres Vives Montpellier, and Pompidou-Metz.

AMANDA LEVETE, Principal of AL_A, is an award-winning architect and designer, who in 2009 formed AL_A following her twenty-year partnership with the late Jan Kaplický at Future Systems.

J. PHILIP O'KANE is Professor Emeritus, and former Dean, Faculty of Engineering, University College Cork; Honorary Fellow, UNESCO-IHE Institute for Water Education (Delft); and Fellow, Irish Academy of Engineers (Dublin), Engineers Ireland (Dublin), and the Royal Society of Arts (London).

SÉAN Ó LAOIRE, architect/urbanist, is past President of the Royal Institute of Architects of Ireland and recipient of the RIAI Triennial Gold Medal. He has collaborated with RFR on a number of (unrealized) projects in Ireland and France.

RENZO PIANO graduated from the Politecnico di Milano. He founded in 1981 the Renzo Piano Building Workshop and is a recipient of the Pritzker Prize, the Sonning Prize, and the AIA Gold Medal. In 2004 he founded the Fondazione Renzo Piano.

MAURICE RICE, Peter's younger brother, is a physicist in condensed matter theory. After studies at UCD and Cambridge University, he worked mainly at Bell Labs in the USA and ETH Zurich in Switzerland. Among his honours are election to the Royal Society UK and the National Academy of Sciences USA.

IAN RITCHIE CBE RA RIBA Hons. RIAS Hons. AIA Hons. DLitt is a director of Ian Ritchie Architects and founding partner with Peter Rice and Martin Francis of RFR.

VIVIENNE ROCHE RHA, born into an engineering family, is a sculptor who has completed commissions for major public works in Dublin and throughout Ireland. She is represented in many public and private collections internationally.

**135**

RICHARD ROGERS, close friend and colleague of Peter Rice, is Chair of Rogers Stirk Harbour + Partners.

ANDY SEDGWICK is an Arup Fellow and a director of Building Engineering in London. He is a specialist in designing with natural light and has particular experience in the museums and galleries field.

JACK ZUNZ F.R.Eng. led the team who designed the Sydney Opera House. Senior Partner at Ove Arup & Partners from 1965, Chairman from 1977 to 1984, Co-Chairman of the Ove Arup Partnership from 1984 to 1989, and first Chairman of the Ove Arup Foundation. He is a recipient of the Gold Medal of the Institution of Structural Engineers.

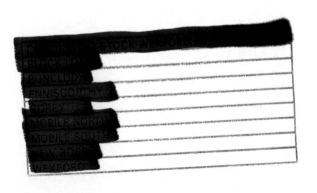

RESPONDING TO what now seems to have
been a pretty far-fetched proposal, I built a ten-
foot-wide model of a footbridge – a spray-painted
jumble of aluminium whose enlargement was
meant to span the Seine. Since it matched his
brightly coloured vision, my Parisian agent was
pleased. He wanted to show it to France's minister
of public works, but first he needed an engineering
opinion. He asked Peter to look at my model.
Surprisingly, Peter showed up.

    'Well, what do you want to know?' he asked
after walking around the maquette a few times.
I thought, 'Oh boy, I'm
really in over my head
now', but managed
to ask as casually as
possible, 'Do you think
it's buildable?' He
looked at the model of
the bridge again and
responded 'Yes.' I didn't
believe him for a second.
Then I began to realize
what that 'Yes' meant.
Sure it was buildable
– buildable by him, not me. But, fortunately, there
was more to it than that. Somehow, even though he
communicated a questioning, perhaps conditional
sense of approval, he did it in such a way that the
recollection makes me happy to this moment. It
seems the 'Yes' implied that the model might be
worth developing if we could work it through; if,
first, I could only make myself clear about my idea
for the bridge.

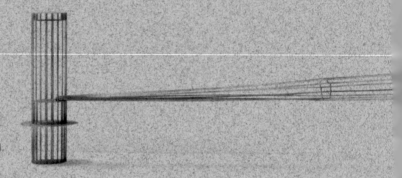

Frank Stella, 'Introduction' to
**Peter Rice, An Engineer Imagines**
(Artemis, London, Zurich, Munich, 1994)